Chick Adventures

Wow Events for Women's Groups

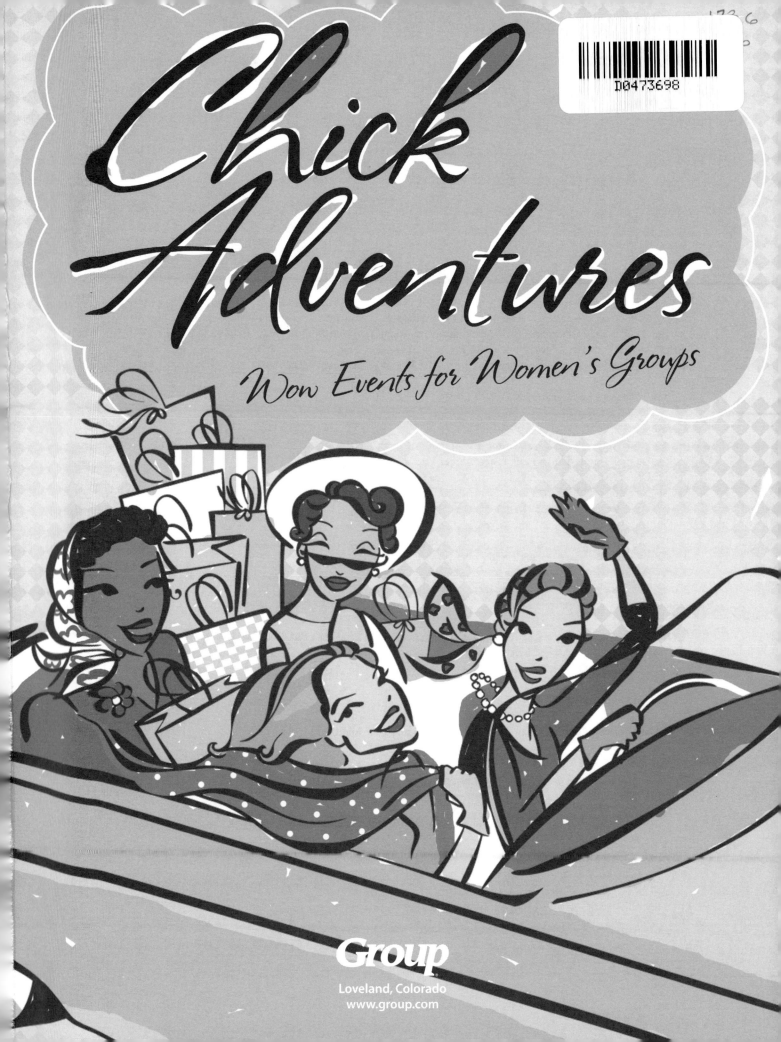

Group

Loveland, Colorado
www.group.com

Chick Adventures: Wow Events for Women's Groups
Copyright © 2007 Group Publishing, Inc.

Visit our Web site: **www.group.com**

Credits
Adventurous Authors: Lisa Biggs Crum, Janna Firestone, Pamela Hall, Angela M. Vomacka, and Billie Wallace
Editor/Safari Guide and Doughnut Taster: Amber Van Schooneveld
Senior Editor and Queen of Chocolate: Amy Nappa
Assistant Editor and Princess of Style: Kate Nickel
Chief Creative Officer/World Adventurer: Joani Schultz
Art Director/Illustrator: Pink Princess Veronica Lucas
Print Production Artists: Greg Longbons and Samantha Wranosky
Cover Art Director: The Amazing Andrea Filer
Cover Designer: The Spectacular Samantha Wranosky
Cover Illustrator Extraordinare: Cindy Luu
Production Manager: DeAnne Lear

Library of Congress Cataloging-in-Publication Data

Chick adventures : wow events for women's groups. -- 1st American pbk. ed.
      p. cm.
  ISBN 978-0-7644-3446-4 (pbk. : alk. paper)
  1. Church work with women. 2. Women in church work. I. Group Publishing.
  BV4445.C55 2007
  259.082--dc22

                           2006100703

ISBN 978-0-7644-3446-4
ISBN 0-7644-3446-2

10 9 8 7 6 5 4 3 2 1   16 15 14 13 12 11 10 09 08 07
Printed in the United States of America.

Contents

Introduction

Are you ready for some fun, refreshing, and new adventures to experience with your friends? This is just the book for you. It's so easy to get in a ministry rut. Have you begun to notice women's eyes drooping as they attend the same ol' tea each year? You know, those standard events where everyone sits at nicely decorated tables, someone gives a devotion, a light meal is served, and then everyone looks under her chair to see if she's got a sticker—because that means she gets to take home the centerpiece. **Well, it's time for something new—get ready for an adventure!**

We've pulled together five fresh, "wow" events to provide women with refreshment, friendship, fun, and an infusion of faith. In fact, we've got you covered for the whole year! In the spring, women will serve others as they complete gardening projects together. In the summer, they'll set sail for a relaxing and renewing day aboard the Port Paradise Cruise. In the fall, they'll have a ball cooking together. In the winter, treat women with a grand Christmas event that offers so much more than tea! And the Girls' Day Out Shopping Adventure is a fun event any time of year.

Women are constantly giving of their time and hearts. The more they give, the greater their need is to be replenished. Jesus taught his followers the importance of getting rest when feeling weary or carrying heavy burdens (Matthew 11:28). And Jesus was intentional about getting away—he and his disciples intentionally went away together for times of rest and renewal (Mark 6:31). Your wow events will be unique ways to replenish women as you take them on adventures. Women will be renewed in God's love and refreshed in friendships with each other. And they'll have a whole lot of fun in the process!

We've planned all five of these events, doing the work so you don't have to! And these ideas are tested with real women—just like you—so we know they work.

In the Book

With each chapter you'll find a fresh new idea, and all the instructions on how to pull it off. Each section guides you in recruiting a team to help you with this event—since none of us can do this alone! You'll also find a timeline to guide you in planning what needs to be accomplished and when. Sections also provide information on what happens at the event, along with a suggested schedule—which you can adapt based on your needs.

Along with these basics, you'll find all kinds of info on decorating, gifts for the women who attend, publicity ideas, what to do during the event, devotions, and more. Read the whole section before you start. It's all here for you!

On the CD-ROM

Pop the CR-ROM included with this book into your computer. You'll see that we've created all kinds of helpful resources to make your event easier! You'll find customizable invitations. There's clip art so you can let your creativity run wild—make posters, T-shirt logos, bulletin inserts, water bottle labels...whatever you want! And we've included helpful instructions and handouts on the CD-ROM to make your event a breeze. Print these on your church copier, or take the disk to your local printing store and have them print what you need.

Other Things to Consider

Child Care

Do you offer it or not? Having child care can often determine whether or not women choose to attend. Here are some ideas for how to handle child care for your event.

- First, check with your church staff to make sure you follow any policies they have regarding child care. Do they require background checks? payment through the church office? Are rooms for child care available? Be sure to support any policies your church has.

- Ask the men's ministry at your church to provide child care during your event. This lets the men show support of moms who need a break.

- Talk to your youth pastor to see if the youth group can provide child care. Suggest it as a ministry opportunity or a fundraiser.

- Ask a campus ministry group at a nearby college if they can provide child care at your event.

- Ask a women's group from another church or Christian organization, and then return the favor.

• Provide professional sitter services.

Be sure to discuss the compensation details with the child care providers before including the "child care provided" statement in your promotional material. Pre-registration for group child care is helpful in planning the number of caregivers, activities, and type of facilities needed. Don't be afraid to charge a small fee for those needing child care. Most parents will pay for it without any hesitation. However, you may choose to cover a portion of the costs through your ministry budget.

 *Setting a Budget*

Speaking of a budget—it's a good idea to have one for your event! Most women's ministries are self-funding. That means you let the women attending share in the cost of the event. That's probably the first thing you need to determine: Will you be paying for this out of the church budget, or will you charge women to attend?

Most people expect to pay to attend events, especially if food is included. You can always supplement with budgeted money, but do consider charging a fee, even if it's small. It helps women commit to the event and lets you plan better, as you'll know how many will be coming.

Things you might need to consider in your budget…

• transportation

• printing of posters, invitations, or announcements

• postage

• food

• decorations

• crafts

• appreciation gifts for volunteers

It's always a good idea to budget an extra 10 percent as "fluff." It always comes in handy for last minute incidentals. In your first meeting with your team members, go over your budget. Let the ladies on your team know at this time what the procedure will be for them to be reimbursed for their expenses.

Girls' Day Out Shopping Adventure

*"Come to me, all of you who are weary and carry heavy burdens, and
I will give you rest" (Matthew 11:28).*

Remember the fun of road trips? OK—leave out the "are we there yet?" parts. But seriously, isn't it freeing to get into the car and drive, especially if you're laughing with friends and sharing about your lives in the process?

This wow event captures the experience of being together with friends, mixes in a favorite pastime of many women—shopping—and provides a spiritual uplift as well. Women will travel together to a fun shopping location, enjoy lunch with friends, and participate in a time of encouragement based on Jesus' promise of rest in Matthew 11:28. Everyone will go home with renewed minds and refreshed spirits.

Your event is divided into four parts: check-in, travel, shopping, and a program. The day begins with check-in at a centralized location such as the church. You travel together to the shopping location by buses, vans, or cars. On the way to the location, the women participate in icebreakers and fun activities that help them get to know one another and begin connecting. At the shopping location, the women are on their own with friends for a few hours. Everyone then regroups at a designated time and location for a meal and an inspiring time together. Make your event a half-day or full-day event based on your needs!

Getting Started

How to Develop Your Event Team

It's no fun to plan an event by yourself, so we suggest you gather a team of eight women. Yes, you can combine some of the jobs on the team if you have a smaller group, but having eight will make the job easier for everyone.

Clearly communicate responsibilities and what you expect from the team. At your first meeting, the Event Coordinator will review each role. In future meetings, referring back to these descriptions will help your team stay on task. It's also helpful to include a tentative schedule for future team meetings.

The following is a list of job descriptions for an eight-girlfriend team. Review these descriptions and modify them according to your event needs.

Event Coordinator: This is the "in-charge" person. She'll direct and manage Girls' Day Out. In fact, if you're reading this book, you're probably the one who is going to take this role! The Event Coordinator

- schedules team meetings and sets each meeting's agenda.
- works with the team to develop the event schedule.
- finalizes the event location.
- leads the devotion experience during the event.
- writes thank you notes to all team members and verifies that all event and financial issues are completed.

Registration Coordinator: This is the person who gets everyone signed up and ready to go. The Registration Coordinator

- organizes event registration.
- determines when and where registration will be held.
- manages all facility needs including getting tables and chairs for registration and appropriate signage.
- recruiting and scheduling volunteers to help with registration.
- develops a registration database and provides a participant list to the event team.
- collects and turns in all fees.

Helpful Hint

Matching jobs with skills and gifts is a great way to go. Let the person who's great at making lists and planning do just that. Invite the woman who loves to cook to be your Food Coordinator. It's so much easier to volunteer if you're able to use a skill or ability you've already got!

Activities Coordinator: This is the job for an upbeat, "cheerleader" personality. She'll organize travel and program activities. The Activities Coordinator

- plans the icebreakers, travel activities, and discussions. (Don't worry—we've got all of this for you in the pages that follow!)
- recruits team captains for each vehicle to lead activities.
- selects and prepares the gift bags, "Girls' Day Out Devotion" cards, and "Today I Pray" cards. (Info on all this is included, too!)

Check-In Coordinator: Here's a job for a friendly and organized person. She's responsible for

- check-in on Saturday morning at the church or a central location.
- recruiting other greeters and helpers as needed.
- preparing sign-in sheets, name tags, and information folders.

Food Coordinator: Here's a job we all think is important! The Food Coordinator

- organizes all meals or snacks.
- plans two menus (for a boxed breakfast and lunch).
- takes care of purchasing, preparing, and setting up breakfast items.
- selects and reserves the restaurant or banquet facility at the event location for the lunch and devotional time.

Transportation Coordinator: This event will flop if no one takes charge of getting everyone on the road! The Transportation Coordinator

- researches transportation options and manages all transportation needs.
- checks charter or rental prices and serves as contact for the charter or rental companies if that option is chosen.
- recruits women to drive if a rental or charter is not chosen.
- manages all financial issues related to transportation expenses.

Promotions Coordinator: This is the job for a woman who loves to talk! The Promotions Coordinator

- handles all publicity for your event.

- handles printing or copying brochures, flyers, postcards, or letters.
- coordinate all mailings, announcements, and other publicity efforts. (Be sure to check out the CD-ROM for all kinds of help with this job!)

Prayer Coordinator: Every event needs lots of prayer! The Prayer Coordinator

- recruits a team of women to pray for the event. This team should be separate from the event team.
- develops a prayer list and forwards it to the event team and prayer team.
- meets with the prayer team for prayer a few times before the event and on Saturday morning before leaving.

Timeline

Eight weeks before your event

- Begin praying for your Girls' Day Out event.
- Read through this chapter in its entirety.
- Develop an event team.
- Set the budget.
- Estimate how many women will attend your event, using figures from previous events as a guide. This will help you determine transportation and meeting room needs.

Seven weeks before your event

- Have a first meeting with your event team. At this meeting:
  - Go over role descriptions and this outline of events.
  - Select when and where to host your event.
  - Discuss transportation.
  - Decide on publicity.
  - Decide whether you'll charge a participant's fee.
  - Decide whether you'll provide child care.
  - Decide who will be responsible for obtaining and setting up tables for check-in and the boxed breakfast.

 ## Six weeks before the event

- Launch publicity.

- Begin event registration.

- The Event Coordinator recruits teams as necessary.

- The Transportation Coordinator reserves transportation.

- The Food Coordinator reserves the banquet facility or restaurant where you'll host lunch or your program.

 ## Four weeks before the event

- Continue publicity and registration.

- The Event Coordinator prepares for the program devotional.

- The Activities Coordinator and her team prepare activities.

- The Food Coordinator selects menus.

 ## Two weeks before the event

- Mail or e-mail reminders to registered participants.

- The Transportation Coordinator confirms transportation for the event.

- The Check-In Coordinator prepares information folders and gathers check-in supplies.

 ## The Day Arrives

- 7:30 . . . . Check-in

- 8:00-10:00 . . . . . Travel to shopping location*

- 10:00-12:30 . . . . Free time to shop

- 12:30-2:00 . . . . . Lunch and program at designated location

- 2:00-4:00 . . . . . . Travel home*

*Time will vary depending on the distance from your location.

Two weeks after your event

- Gather your team for an appreciation party. It shows how grateful you are, and helps them want to sign up for your next event!

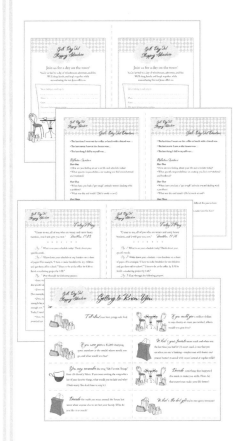

Let's Get Planning!

∽ Where to Go ∽

Whether you live in the city, suburbs, or country, there are probably several good shopping locations for your event. If you're from a smaller town, make a trip to the big city. If you're from the big city, find a small town with a downtown shopping area for a change of pace.

To choose the best location, brainstorm with your event team. Keep in mind who'll be participating in your event. Is your target audience women from all ages and stages or a niche group such as moms, single women in their 30s, or women in the marketplace? Research your various options before making a final decision on the location.

When researching the location, find out if any other activities are happening on the same day as your event, such as fairs or festivals. Smaller towns often sponsor special weekends for women that include contests, giveaways, or games. These can be fun activities to add into your excursion, and the best part is that you and your team don't have to plan them.

You can even get outside the box with shopping locations. Maybe you have some women who love antiquing or visiting garage sales. Visit areas rich with the types of shops that will appeal to your ladies.

∽ When to Go ∽

Your shopping event can be held anytime throughout the year. Consider two questions: When is the best time of the year for the women in your church to get away? What are the potential scheduling conflicts? Talking with your event team is essential because "plans go wrong for lack of advice; but many counselors bring success" (Proverbs 15:22). If a team isn't in place when you are scheduling your event, survey a *small* group of women from the ages and stages of your target audience. Gathering information from a group will help you make an informed decision and avoid potential scheduling problems. Remember, time conflicts or prior commitments will prevent some from attending. Choose a day that works for the majority of women. (It's just a fact of life that no day will work for *everyone*.)

Think about hosting the event at a time of the year when women need a break, such as the fall after the kids are back in school or, if weather permits, in the winter following a busy Christmas season. If you schedule a spring event, check school schedules to avoid conflicts with spring breaks or end of the year school activities. Summer is a great time, especially for moms who need a break from being with their children all day. Don't plan your event on a weekend when other church activities are scheduled, especially a men's event if dads are needed to care for the children.

How to Get There

 ### Travel Time and Schedule

When choosing the location of your event, it's important to consider the amount of time required for travel. Stay within two hours of your community if possible. Women will be reluctant to invest more than four hours traveling even for a fun shopping trip. Also allow time for check-in, which might require the ladies to arrive 30 minutes prior to leaving. The following is a recommended scheduled for hosting your event.

Schedule

7:30 . . . . Check-in

8:00-10:00 . . . . . Travel to shopping location*

10:00-12:30 . . . . Free time to shop

12:30-2:00 . . . . . Lunch and program at a designated location

2:00-4:00 . . . . . . Travel home*

*Time will vary depending on the distance from your location.

 ### Transportation

You'll need to determine how your group will travel to and from the shopping location. If you have a large group, consider chartering buses. It's convenient and allows a larger number of women to connect. Research local charter companies, and get a reference from other ministries who have used their services. Arrange for the buses to arrive at least 30 minutes before you are scheduled to leave. The women will need to begin boarding 15 minutes

Alternate Schedule
If you want to adjust your schedule to allow women more time to shop and be with friends, have women do lunch on their own. Regroup in the afternoon for your program and provide desserts or snacks.

7:15:
Check-in
8:00-10:00:
Travel to shopping location
10:00-2:30:
Free time to shop and lunch on your own
2:30-4:00:
Afternoon snacks and program at a designated location

Helpful Hint

Here's a discussion to have with your event team. Should you assign women to vans and cars, or should you let women choose who they'll ride with? Remember that not everyone has a friend already, and some might feel left out if they're standing aside waiting to be invited into a car. Create a plan so that every woman feels included and befriended.

before your departure time.

Vans are a great option for smaller groups. If you don't have church vans or money budgeted for rental vans, recruit a minivan brigade. Ask a group of women who have minivans to drive and give them a discount on their registration fee or waive it altogether. The women can also drive in cars, but this should be your last choice. Traveling together on a bus or van allows the women an opportunity to interact as a larger group.

Your Transportation Coordinator is responsible for making vehicle assignments and preparing a transportation list prior to the event. If your whole group is traveling together, only one list is necessary. However, if multiple vehicles are used, she needs a list for each vehicle with the names of women traveling on that particular van, bus, or car. The list should have participant names, cell phone numbers, emergency contact numbers, and vehicle assignments.

Before the event, the Activities Coordinator will recruit a "Travel Agent" for each vehicle. These women lead the activities and check participants on the vehicle to make sure no one gets left behind at any time. They should check names at least three times during the event—on Saturday morning prior to leaving, after shopping if you travel to a lunch location, and when returning home. Have your Travel Agents at the buses or vans 15 to 30 minutes before you're scheduled to leave.

Promoting Your Event

Participation in your event will depend on how well you promote it. You should begin promotions around six weeks prior to the trip. Use the customizable promotions material included on the CD-ROM.

- Print out and mail the invitation on the CD-ROM. It's important to get something into the hands of each person.

- Create posters, a bulletin insert, and a PowerPoint slide using the clip art from the CD-ROM.

Promote your event at any women's ministry opportunities including weekly Bible studies, small groups, a mom's ministry, or Sunday school classes. Are you inviting high school and college girls to attend, too? If so, be sure to make announcements at their gatherings. Encourage friends to go on the adventure together. Also promote through other ministries such as small groups or Sunday school classes for men or couples. Imagine how excited the women would be if their husbands encouraged them to participate.

Lastly, word of mouth is the most effective way to persuade women to attend. Everyone involved in the event needs to be promoting it. Challenge the women on your team to invite at least two or three friends and get their friends inviting others as well. Do your best to create a buzz in the church about this fun opportunity just for women.

Sell gift certificates to your event if it's scheduled around a holiday such as Christmas or Mother's Day (use the clip-art on the CD-ROM to make these). They make great gifts, and it's even more special when a woman's friends or family encourage her to take time for herself.

Event Registration

Begin your registration around six weeks before the event. For best results, have a table or booth set up in a central location at your church each Sunday. It's also a good idea to have registration forms available at the church office or a registration table set up when women's Bible studies or small groups are meeting.

The registration team will need registration forms, promotional pieces, pens, and a cash box with change. If you have a table in a central location on Sunday or during the week, use decorations such as balloons or banners to draw women to your table. Remember to put your promotional piece on the table also; it's a quick way for women to find out event details.

Your Registration Coordinator is responsible for the registration database. It should include the participant's name, a phone number, registration fee information (paid or still owes money), the names of friends with whom she wants to travel, and emergency contact numbers. Once the list is finalized, the transportation and Check-In Coordinators will need this information.

Planning Your Meals

Breakfast to Go

Your event will ideally begin early on a Saturday morning. Let women know what meals you're going to provide so they can plan ahead. If your event begins at 8:00 a.m., you should provide a boxed breakfast or snack for the participants. Have your food team purchase the breakfast items. At check-in, set up tables with the food, drinks, plastic ware, napkins, and to-go boxes. The women can choose their breakfast and box it up for the trip. It's quick and convenient.

Recommended Breakfast Menu

- Bananas and apples

- Granola bars

- Cheese sticks

- Assorted yogurts (Don't forget the plastic spoons.)

- Bottled fruit juice and water

Helpful Hint

For fun decorations for your lunch location or gifts for the women, be sure to check out www.group.com/women.

Lunch on Location

The Food Coordinator will be responsible for choosing the location for your lunch and program. You could host it at a restaurant, at a hotel, or at a banquet facility. The lunch menu will be determined by the location chosen. When selecting the type of lunch you want, keep in mind your schedule. If you only have one and a half hours for lunch and a program, a buffet usually works best. Most restaurants or banquet facilities will offer hot and cold buffets. Check with the catering staff for your options. If your group chooses to host the program later in the afternoon, the women will have lunch on their own. You'll need to check with the restaurant or banquet staff for refreshment options and pricing.

When your Food Coordinator makes arrangements with the restaurant or banquet facility for your lunch, she also needs to determine the room set-up. Request round tables that seat 8 to 10 people per table. If round tables aren't available, work with the catering staff to determine the best room set up that will allow small group discussion.

It's Time to Travel!

Getting Ready for Check-In

The women should meet at a central location on Saturday morning for check-in. You'll need between two to four tables and four to six volunteers depending on the size of your group. Plan for your volunteers to arrive at least 30 minutes before check-in begins. Provide an alphabetical registration list, highlighters, and signs indicating where the women are to check-in, e.g. A-L, M-Z. It's also helpful to have one or two greeters who can answer questions.

When the women arrive, members of the check-in team will highlight participant names on the registration list, distribute event folders, and identify the name of each person's Travel Agent and vehicle in which she will be traveling. The folder should include a schedule, name tag, list of shops, and a list of restaurants if the women are lunching on their own. Volunteers will also give out the gift bags and direct ladies to breakfast tables.

Planning Your Activities

Girls' Day Out Shopping Bag

As women check in, wow them with one of these gift bags. It's a fun way to make each person feel welcomed and special. Although you have different options for the gift bag, a great choice is a trendy tote bag with your women's ministry or event logo. When women carry the bags while shopping, it helps them identify other women from the group. It can also generate conversation with other people at the shopping location.

The Activities Coordinator and her team will put together the gift bags. Here are ideas of what you might fill these bags with:

- Prepackaged snacks such as granola bars, crackers, gum, or candy bars
- Bottled water. For extra fun, use the clip art on the CD-ROM and make you own labels for the water bottles.
- Ask local businesses for donations such as coupons or cosmetic samples.
- Lip balm
- Tissue packs

Be creative and have fun preparing bags with gifts women will enjoy!

Travel Time Activities

One of the most fun elements of the Girls' Day Out Shopping Adventure is traveling to your location. Maximize the travel time with activities that will help the women connect. The Activities Coordinator will assign Travel Agents to lead the icebreaker and activities while traveling to the shopping

Helpful Hint

Since the group will be on their own for shopping, get cell phone numbers for the participants. If anyone doesn't show up when you regroup, the Registration or Transportation Coordinator or Travel Agents can give the missing person a call. It's also a good idea to give the participants the Travel Agent's cell phone number. This will help you avoid any misunderstandings and keep on schedule.

Prep

Before the event, print the "Getting to Know You" page from the CD-ROM and make as many copies as you need. Cut the slips apart on the indicated lines, put the slips into a bright little gift bag, and you're ready to go! If you're going to be traveling in cars, put a handful of questions into colorful envelopes instead of a gift bag, and give one envelope to each car's Travel Agent.

Helpful Hint

If you're playing this on a large bus, it will be hard for everyone to hear answers. If you don't have a sound system on the bus, simply have women do this activity in groups of 4 to 6 with those sitting nearby.

location. If you have multiple vehicles, a Travel Agent should be assigned to each vehicle. That group of women will become a team.

The activities you select set the tone for the day. Make the trip there a time of fun and laughter. Shortly after getting underway, have the Activities Coordinator or a Travel Agent introduce herself and explain the purpose for the day. She might say something such as:

Our goal is to have a day out with girlfriends, which means taking a mental break from all your responsibilities. We have a fun icebreaker and activities that will help you laugh and learn something interesting about others. Ecclesiastes 3:4 says "there is a time to laugh," and today is our day! It's time to put your responsibilities behind you and look forward to a fun day with the girls.

Then, have her introduce the icebreaker to get things started.

Getting to Know You Icebreaker

Get women gabbing with these questions—they'll learn some fun details they don't know about each other. Pass the bag or envelope of questions and ask each person to draw one out—without peeking!

Have each person introduce herself and answer her question so everyone can hear. Others can feel free to ask questions to get to know more if they want.

If you're traveling on a large bus, give prizes for the best or most unique answers. Have the women nominate others for a Girls' Day Out Award. Share the category with the whole group, and women can nominate. After the nominees are identified, take a vote and award certificates to the winner in each of the following categories.

- Most Unusual Answer
- Most Hilarious Response
- Most Unforgettable Reply

Team Activities

After the women have connected through the icebreaker, the next two activities are designed to help the women become a team. If your whole group is traveling together, form two or three teams and appoint a Travel Agent for each group. If you're traveling in cars or vans, give these games to the Travel Agent in each vehicle to play with that smaller group. You can do either activity or both depending on your travel distance and personal preference.

Activity 1: That Common Connection

Each team will choose a name and mascot after identifying a common connection. Have Travel Agents lead women in this activity.

Begin by asking, "What do we have in common with each other?" For example, someone might say she loves soaking in a hot tub. Ask the women to raise their hands if they also love the tub. If everyone raises her hand, you have identified something they have in common with each other. If not, continue taking suggestions and surveying until you find a common connection. Help the women think of fun, creative connections, such as hobbies, favorite foods, temperaments, passions.

After identifying your common connection, choose a team name and mascot that best represents your group. For example the women on your team all like to ride bicycles or have gone on mission trips. Your name might be "Biker Chicks" or "Mission-Minded Mamas." After choosing your name, ask for a volunteer who would be willing to dress up as your mascot. Collect items from the women for her outfit and do a dress rehearsal. Encourage women to get out of the box with the mascot costumes and have fun with it! Everyone will have to be creative since you won't be bringing any props along—costumes will be created with what's on hand in the car or bus.

Later in the day, the Travel Agents will introduce the teams, share their common connection, and then introduce their mascots. (Mascots need to slip out immediately after lunch to get prepared.) Prizes will be awarded to the favorite team!

After you've chosen mascots, have teams discuss these questions:

- When was the last time you found a common connection with someone that you didn't expect?
- How did it help you open up with that person and get to know her?
- How does focusing on our common connections deepen our relationships?

On the Bus?

If you're riding in a bus, grab a Throw & Tell Ice-Breakers ball from Group. Women can toss the ball back and forth on the bus; then the woman who catches it answers whatever question her right thumb lands on. Get ready for laughter! Visit www.group.com.

Scavenger Hunt Lists

Relax Basket

(Provide a basket for these items.)

bubble bath
candle
lighter
magazine
chocolates
a pretty washcloth

Tea for Two

(Provide a small teapot to hold these items.)

assorted teas

shortbread cookies
a card or invitation for a friend
a box of scone mix
strawberry jam or lemon curd
two teacups

A Walk in the Park

(Provide a small fanny pack to hold these items.)

water bottle
pedometer
visor or cap
healthy snack
sunscreen
a fun music CD

Activity 2: Team Scavenger Hunt

When the women arrive at the shopping location, they'll be on their own or with friends for a few hours. Why not use that time to help them stay connected by hosting a team scavenger hunt?

The Activities Coordinator will provide a list of scavenger hunt items. Each Travel Agent will be given a copy of the list and an envelope with individual items written on strips of paper. Have the team members choose the strips of paper to discover what one item they'll need to find while shopping. When everyone regroups for lunch, the women will give their items to the Travel Agent. She presents their scavenger hunt items at the program and the winning team is announced. It's a fun competition, especially if you choose Travel Agents that like to ham it up. Give members of the winning team discount coupons to an upcoming women's ministry event.

Most women love door prizes, so why not choose scavenger hunt items that when combined become a door prize for your event? If you have multiple vehicles, have separate scavenger hunt lists with a variety of themes. When the items are collected, have each group put together their door prize to be given away at the afternoon program. It's important to keep the cost of each item under $5. If an item is more, have two women get the item.

Day Out Devotion

The goal of Girls' Day Out is to help women be refreshed and renewed. Travel time activities and shopping with friends provide a fun break, but your program is an essential part of the event, too. Not only will women have fun, they'll also leave inspired and encouraged to take time for themselves. Your program will give women practical tips on how to find rest in Jesus every day.

Food First

Welcome women, and have them find seats. Thank God for the food and the time together, and then enjoy your meal or dessert, depending on which is being served.

Now For Fun!

Begin with the Common Connection team activity. The Event Coordinator can be emcee, or ask someone else to fill this role. Introduce the Travel Agents, and have them identify their teams and introduce their mascots. Let the Travel Agent share the common connection and explain how the team mascot represents their group. After all the mascots are introduced, the judges decide which mascot best represents her team. Remember, the winning team receives a goody bag for the trip home.

If you chose to do the team Scavenger Hunt, have the Travel Agents present the items collected as you read the item list. Encourage teams to cheer as they present their items. The team with the most items from their list can receive prizes such as coupons to future women's ministry events. Then have the Activities Coordinator and her team group the items into your themed door prizes. You can distribute the door prizes as you wish—to the team who bought the most items, to the winning Common Connection team, or to women whose names are drawn.

Once the travel time activities are completed, it's time to share the Day Out Devotion.

Devotion

Begin by having women complete the first three sentences on the "Girls' Day Out Devotion" cards together. These are the sentences they'll complete:

• The last time I went out for coffee or lunch with a friend was…

• The last movie I saw at the theater was…

• The last thing I did by myself was…

After they've had time to discuss, do a quick survey of the group. Ask the women to raise their hands and answer the following questions.

 **Let's see how well you did. How many of you have done coffee or lunch with a friend in the last week? The last six weeks? The last three months?**

Helpful Hint
Three members from your event team can serve as judges to select the best team mascot.

Day Out Devotion Prep
The Activities Coordinator and her team will need to prepare two items for the devotion, the "Today I Pray" card and the "Girls' Day Out Devotion" card.
• Print one "Today I Pray" card from the CD-ROM for each attendee, and have them laminated at your church office or a local print shop.
• Print out the "Girls' Day Out Devotion" card and have one at each table.

How many of you have gone to a movie in the last week, six weeks, or three months?

How many of you have done something by yourself in the last week, six weeks, or three months?

Reflect for a moment. What do your answers reveal about you? Pause. **Is your life so busy that you are forgetting to take any time for refreshment? If so, you're not alone. We've all been there. We've all struggled to find balance between caring for others and caring for ourselves.**

Give women 10 minutes to read the first two reflection questions from the devotion cards and answer them together at their tables. Here are the questions:

• How are you feeling about your life and schedule today?

• What specific responsibilities are making you feel overwhelmed and burdened?

SAY: **No one understands the struggle to balance responsibilities better than Jesus. Have you ever given much thought to what Jesus' schedule was like? It wasn't unusual for him to go to bed late and to get up early. People constantly went to him for help. When he wasn't teaching the crowds, he was teaching his disciples. He must have experienced the same temptations we do—the temptation to neglect ourselves when caring for others and the temptation to neglect our relationship with God because we think we don't have time for it.**

Jesus overcame these temptations by being intentional, and he taught his followers to do the same. In Matthew 11:28, he told them, "Come to me, all of you who are weary and carry heavy burdens, and I will give you rest."

Let's be honest. Most of us are familiar with this verse, but we don't do very well practicing it. When we are feeling weary and burdened, the place to begin is Jesus. Yet, so often he is our last resort. Instead of going to him, we try to handle the circumstances on our own. We adopt a "get tough" attitude and say to ourselves, "I will get through this even if it kills me." We dig in and get tough just to get through it.

Have women discuss the next two reflection questions from the devotion card at their tables:

• When have you had a "get tough" attitude toward dealing with a problem?

• What was the end result? (Did it work or not?)

SAY: The "get tough" attitude requires sacrifices that God isn't asking us to make. We sacrifice our relationship with him. We sacrifice our relationship with the people in our lives. At best, we become grumpy because we're not getting enough rest. At worst, we become resentful because people don't understand how hard we're working. In making the wrong sacrifices, we sacrifice our own physical, emotional, and spiritual well-being. God's solution to your schedule isn't to sacrifice yourself. His solution is to get intentional about spending time with Jesus.

Jesus repeatedly went to his Father to talk with him about the issues he was facing and the burdens he was carrying. After spending time with God, he always knew how to handle his circumstances. He was able to continue his fast paced, hectic schedule. He was never resentful of the crowds or their needs. He was inwardly refreshed and renewed.

If Jesus needed that time, then it's also essential for us. Life will always be busy. We have to get intentional about how we are going to respond to it. Choosing to dig in and get tough isn't the solution. It means we are choosing to carry our burdens alone. It also means we are heading toward burn out rather than experiencing daily refreshment and renewal.

Jesus' solution is "Come to me… I will give you rest." He could have expressed it this way, "When you come to me, I will help you. I will give you strength to face your day. As you give me your burdens, I'll give you rest and refreshment in return. By coming to me, you acknowledge your need and recognize that you can't do it alone."

Have women discuss the last two reflection questions on the devotion cards at their tables:

• What are the obstacles that make it difficult for you to have time with Jesus?

• What step can you take this week to make time for him?

SAY: To help you apply this, we have something for you to take home, a "Today I Pray" card. Each morning for the next two weeks, we want you to use this card to pray about your daily needs. It will only take about 10 minutes of your day. It's designed to help you get intentional about coming to Jesus and to get specific about your schedule and daily needs.

Distribute the "Today I Pray" cards, and review them with the women and explain how they'll use it.

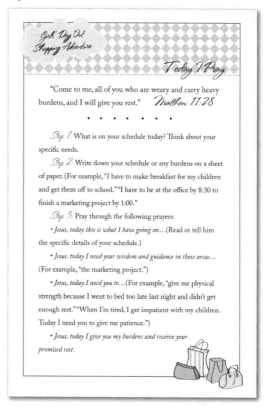

After reviewing the prayer card, close in prayer, thanking God that he is our rest, that he will carry our burdens, and that we can always come to him. Pray that each woman will remember daily to go to Jesus for rest.

Day Out Closing

Close your program by enthusiastically thanking each woman who came. Make sure to also acknowledge the team of volunteers who served and present them with appreciation gifts (these could be the themed scavenger hunt gifts, as a surprise). This is also a good time to let ladies know about any upcoming Bible studies or events you have planned for women's ministry.

Celebrating Your Success

Schedule a celebration party two to four weeks after your event. Review comments you've heard and get feedback from your team about what worked well and what needs to be done differently. Celebrate your success with dessert and coffee. Most importantly, spend time in prayer celebrating *with* God what he did in and through your team. Enjoy yourself because you did a great job planning your event—take a day out yourself!

Seeds of Friendship Gardening Party

"Jesus said, 'How can I describe the Kingdom of God? What story should I use to illustrate it? It is like a mustard seed planted in the ground. It is the smallest of all seeds, but it becomes the largest of all garden plants; it grows long branches, and birds can make nests in its shade'"
(Mark 4:30-32).

The smell of soil after a good rain, a warm breeze on the air, the twitter of birds in the morning. These can only mean one thing: It's spring planting time! In this wow event, women will get dirt under their fingernails as they serve others in the church and community. They'll bless women in your community by helping with garden projects, *and* they'll plant seeds of friendship with one another while working away.

Women will gather at your church for refreshments and a short devotion, get into Garden Groups of six, and then be off to multiple garden projects. They'll spend the rest of the event in their Garden Groups—enjoying getting to know each other better, serving, and learning gardening tips from others in the group. And to make it a memorable day for all involved, you'll sprinkle your event with surprises to delight the women.

Read the verse above. The smallest of seeds becomes long branches and a home for birds. Part of the joy in gardening is these surprises God has planted in the world around us. Throughout your event, you'll remind women of the "surprises of joy" God has placed in the world around them and in their friendships with one another.

Use this four-hour event to bring the women in your ministry closer together, to touch the lives of others, and be an inviting and safe event for first-time visitors.

Getting Started

During this event, women will be placed into groups of six called Garden Groups. It will help everyone make new friends. And, since each woman has a specific role in her Garden Group, it makes each woman feel important.

You'll need to recruit a leader for each group, the Garden Guru. Her role, and all the other Garden Group roles are explained in detail later in the chapter, but for now keep in mind that you'll be placing women in these groups later in your planning process.

Your Root Team

These women will be the roots of your event. You want to enjoy the event, too, so develop and recruit a team of women to share responsibilities. As women agree to be on the Root Team, be sure to exchange e-mail addresses. E-mailing your Root Team with updates throughout the planning time can replace unnecessary and hard-to-schedule meetings. But even if your Root Team is great at keeping in touch, schedule at least two face-to-face meetings with your Root Team prior to the event.

Director: This will more than likely be *you*! This person is organized and detailed, and will uphold the vision of the event to provide friendship and fun for women. She'll read this chapter in its entirety, recruit the Root Team, and ensure all steps are followed for a successful event. By modeling the servant leader, she'll step in wherever needed. This woman will also recruit two women to be registration table attendants the morning of the event, and she'll emcee the morning program.

Publicity and Sign-Up Leader: This woman will coordinate all publicity efforts and collect names and information of the women signing up for the event. She'll assign women to be the Garden Gurus for each group. She'll also create and present a celebration slide show the Sunday after your event. See the "Publicity and Sign-Up" section.

Helpful Hint
Feel free to ask another woman to direct this event. Provide an opportunity for someone on your women's ministry team to grow through leading. And, this will provide you the opportunity to attend, get to know some of the ladies in your ministry better, and enjoy.

Lead Garden Guru: This woman is an experienced gardener, and will choose the gardening projects for your event. She'll find out who in the church and community could use help in their gardens. She may seek out these people, receive recommendations from others in the church, or make announcements for prospective hostesses to sign up. She'll also be the contact person for each group's Garden Guru, communicating project information and telling each Garden Guru what supplies she'll need to gather. See the "Seeds of Friendship Gardening Ideas" section for more information.

The Stage Setter: This woman loves adding those extra touches to make an event special. She'll plan the setup and decorations for the morning program of the event. She will also provide the refreshments as the women arrive at the church the morning of the event and plan the lunches. See the "Refreshments and Lunch" section and the "Setting the Stage" section for instructions and ideas.

Timeline

Ten weeks before your event

- Begin praying for your Seeds of Friendship event.

- Read through this chapter in its entirety.

- Recruit your Root Team.

- Estimate how many women will attend your event, using figures from previous retreats or women's events as a guide. This will help you finalize location details and will determine how many projects the Lead Gardening Guru should find.

Nine weeks before your event

- Meet with your Root Team. (You may want your Root Team to read this chapter before the meeting.) At this meeting:

  - Choose the event date and place.

  - Go over Root Team role descriptions and this outline of your event.

  - Decide on publicity. (See the "Publicity and Sign-Up" section.)

Helpful Hint
If you have a large women's ministry group, you can lighten each woman's load by sharing Root Team roles.

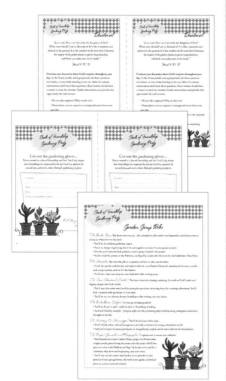

- Set a budget, determining how much money the Stage Setter and Garden Gurus will have to work with.

  - Decide whether you'll charge a participant's fee.

  - Decide whether you'll provide child care.

- Reserve the room in which you'll host the event for that day and the day before for setup.

Eight weeks before your event

- Launch publicity.

- Begin signing women up for your event.

- The Lead Garden Guru begins finding gardening projects.

Six weeks before your event

- Continue publicity and registration.

- The Publicity and Sign-Up Leader keeps a close eye on how women are signing up for the event, and begins asking women who've indicated garden experience to be Garden Gurus for each group.

- The Publicity and Sign-Up Leader stays in close communication with the Lead Garden Guru regarding how many garden projects will be necessary.

- The Lead Garden Guru begins finalizing gardening projects.

Four weeks before your event

- The Lead Garden Guru should have final projects chosen. She makes site visits to the hostesses' homes to evaluate the projects and make a list of supplies needed for each project.

- The Lead Garden Guru assigns a project to each group's Garden Guru and communicates the project to each Garden Guru, including directions and contact information.

- If you decide to provide child care, arrange it with your children's ministry and nursery directors. (See the introduction for child care tips.)

- Request time in the morning services on the Sunday following the event or at your next women's ministry event for a celebration slide show.

- The Stage Setter begins planning and gathering decorations for the event and chooses her morning refreshment menu and plans lunch.

- Request any technical support you'll need for the event, such as a sound system and microphone.

Two weeks to one week before your event

- The Publicity and Sign-Up Leader may send an e-mail reminder to women registered for the event, reminding them to each bring a trowel.

- The Director recruits two women to be registration attendants.

- Continue publicity and registration.

The week of your event

- Don't forget to keep praying!

- The Director reads through and prepares for the morning program's devotional.

- The Publicity and Sign-Up Leader along with the Director assign women to Garden Groups, leaving a couple of empty spots on each team for late registrants.

- The Stage Setter gathers supplies, food, and beverages for the morning program.

- The Garden Gurus contact their hostesses to confirm projects. (The hostesses are the women whose gardens you'll be working on.) They also gather the gardening supplies their groups will need.

The day before your event

- The Stage Setter and the Root Team set up the meeting room.

- The Director prints out devotion handouts and Garden Group roles, and has them available at each Garden Group's table.

It's Gardening Day!

Here's an overview of what's going to happen the day of your event:

- **8:00 a.m.** Root Team arrives at church to set out morning refreshments, pray over the event, turn the music on, and troubleshoot any

Helpful Hint

Adjust this sample schedule based on how close the hostesses live to the church. Allow plenty of time for transportation.

last-minute challenges. The Publicity and Sign-Up Leader should be available during registration to reassign Garden Groups or roles as necessary.

- **8:45 to 9:00 a.m.** Registration (As each woman arrives, greet her with a welcoming smile. Ask her name, check her off the list, and confirm with her which Garden Group she's in, what role she has, and what her responsibilities are.)

- **9:00 to 9:15 a.m.** Greeting and refreshments

- **9:15 to 9:30 a.m.** Devotional

- **9:30 to 10:00 a.m.** Groups travel from church to hostess homes

- **10:00 a.m. to 12:00 p.m.** Garden Projects

- **12:00 to 12:30 p.m.** Lunch and Devotional Questions

- **12:30 to 1:00 p.m.** Groups travel back to church, and share insights with the Reaper, who leaves her notes with the Publicity and Sign-Up Leader.

- **1:00 to 2:00 p.m.** Root Team cleans up

The week after your event

- The Garden Guru e-mails pictures from their gardening sites to the Publicity and Sign-Up Leader.

- The Director hosts a thank you coffee time with the Root Team and evaluates how the event went and how you can improve it for the next year.

The Sunday after your event

- Show the celebration slide show at your church service or women's ministry event.

The Garden Groups

We mentioned earlier that women are in Garden Groups of six. Women will dig deeper into friendships by spending the day in these groups. Each Garden Group will have one gardening project to work on together. Before the event you'll need to find a Garden Guru to serve as the leader for each group. The remaining members of each group will choose roles among themselves the day of the event. Here's a description of the roles:

Celebration Slide Show

Always celebrate what women experience at your great events. In your Celebration Slide Show, you'll share the moments photographers captured throughout the event. The Publicity and Sign-Up Leader will put your show to music, and share it at your church service or women's event the following week. She can also share stories from the event, which the journalers have recorded. This will not only celebrate and appreciate the women who participated, but show others what they can be involved in. For the next event, they may be the first to sign up!

The Garden Guru: You know who she is…She *already* has dirt under her fingernails, and daisies seem to spring up wherever her feet land.

- This woman will be your resident gardening expert. The Lead Garden Guru will have communicated beforehand the nature of the project, directions to the hostess's house, and contact information.

- She'll be in charge of gathering the tools and supplies necessary for her group's project.

- She'll call the hostess the week of the event to confirm the project.

- On-site, she'll provide kind guidance as the group completes the project.

- She'll bring a digital camera for the Reaper on her team to take pictures of their project, and e-mail the pictures to the Publicity and Sign-Up Leader after the event for the Celebration Slide Show.

The Nourisher: This woman has the gift of hospitality.

- She'll pick up the sack lunches and water bottles for her Garden Group the morning of the event, one for each group member and one for the hostess.

- She'll also make sure everyone stays hydrated.

The Sower (Devotional Leader): This woman has a heart for sharing, scattering the seeds of God's truth, and digging deeper into God's truths.

- She'll spur discussion over lunch by asking key questions stemming from the morning's devotional. We've provided devotional questions for her on the CD-ROM, which she'll get the morning of the event.

- She'll be sure to cultivate deeper friendships while working and talking over lunch.

The Wheelbarrow (Helper): This is the woman whose joy is to help others.

- She'll be your go-to girl—ready to pitch in if anything is lacking.

- And she'll lead by example—jumping right into the gardening project and spurring contagious excitement throughout the day.

- *Gardening Site Supplies*
- *Your Garden Gurus will be in charge of gathering the tools needed for her team. But you can ask each woman to bring her own trowel to the event. Here are some of the things the Garden Guru will probably need to gather:*
  - *digital camera*
  - *garden fork*
  - *shovel*
  - *hoe*
  - *rake*
  - *potting soil*
  - *flowers, seeds, plants, small trees, shrubs*
  - *watering can*
  - *planters and containers (for container gardening)*
  - *wheelbarrow or cart*

Helpful Hint

What if the numbers don't work out...six women per group? We all know plans change. Plan ahead to be flexible the morning of the event. Allow those who sign up late to take the place of those who couldn't make it. You can combine roles, such as the Watering Can and the Wheelbarrow, if you have too few women.

Helpful Hint

If you're new to gardening, here are some suggested resources:
- *The Home Depot Flower Gardening 1-2-3*
- *Better Homes and Gardens New Complete Guide to Gardening*
- *Gardening for Dummies*

The Watering Can (Encourager): This woman is the heart of the team.

- She'll refresh others with encouragement and rally excitement by being a cheerleader of all.
- And she'll ensure everyone participates in the gardening project and no one is left out of conversation.

The Reaper (journaler and photographer): Capture each moment and celebrate!

- She'll journal about her Garden Group's project. She'll write what insights people gained during the project with her Garden Group after their project. She'll then give her notes to the Publicity and Sign-Up Leader to be used for a celebration slide show and for planning next year's event.
- This woman will use the camera the Garden Guru provides to take pictures of her group, her hostess, the work in the garden, individual pictures, and moments of ministry.

Let's Get Planning!

∽ Whom Should We Serve? ∽

Just about any woman would love to have a group come over and renovate her garden! Here are a few ideas of whom to consider as a hostess who would be served by this event. They could be women in your church or women in your community. Think of anyone who could use some extra hands in the garden.

- A mother who has just had a baby

- A woman who has physical challenges preventing her from weeding and doing some of the bigger gardening projects, but who is able to get around to water the flowers

- A woman planning an outside wedding and wanting to get some flowers planted to decorate

- A woman who has just moved (from within the town or from out-of-town) and would appreciate help getting a jump on her garden

- The church's receptionist or administrative assistant. Really, any church staff giving tirelessly of themselves. What a way to thank her!

- A woman who has been going through a rough time, such as a personal or family illness. Use the event to encourage and uplift her.

- A mother planning a backyard graduation party for her child. With all the excitement and preparation, it's time-consuming to take care of the garden as well.

- Your projects don't have to be limited to homes. You could also do garden projects for a local shelter, a nursing home, a not-for-profit company, your church, or a day-care center.

~ *Seeds of Friendship Project Ideas* ~

Here are a few project ideas for six women to do in the two-hour time-frame. Of course, there are many factors affecting how long each project will take. Rely on the Gardening Guru to estimate the timeframe on each project. And make sure the Gardening Guru is cautious when approaching prospective hostesses. Don't say, "We've noticed that your garden could use some help." Rather say, "We know your life is busy, and you might need some help. We're planning some Garden Groups on [state specific day] and were wondering if you could use some extra hands as you work in your garden. There's no charge to you at all—it's our gift to you!"

- Weed and plant a garden. Depending on the condition of the soil and number of weeds, a 30-square-foot garden is doable for six women in two hours. Rely on the expertise of the Gardening Guru to evaluate whether the amount of weeding can be done in the time allotted.

- Container gardening. The hostess might have flower boxes outside her windows or flowerpots in her backyard. Be sure the Garden Guru asks her what her favorite flowers are and what colors she likes.

Budget Saving Tips

- *Shop sales and clearance items.*
- *Borrow tools rather than purchasing them.*
- *Call nurseries eight weeks in advance and let them know what your church is planning. They may have overstock of certain items that they would be able to sell at a discount or even donate.*
- *Call groceries and delis in advance to ask for discounts and possibly donations of lunch items.*
- *Shop flea markets and garage sales for unique and inexpensive containers for container gardening.*
- *Charge a nominal registration fee for the event.*
- *Ask for containers or mulch donations from church members.*

Make a container garden for her to brighten each day! This could also include an herb garden. Many home improvement stores or gardening shops carry pots with multiple openings just right for a variety of herbs in each pot.

- Prepare and hang flowerpots. Another way to brighten someone's front porch or back patio is to hang flowerpots. Again, be sure to include the hostess' favorite flowers and colors for this project.

- Plant a few small trees or shrubs. If the hostess is in a new home and needs to establish landscaping, it would be helpful to plant trees and shrubs for her.

- If a team is extremely efficient and finishes the projects early, think of additional things to do for the hostess such as sweeping the porch, washing the front door, wiping down lawn furniture, organizing a garden bench, or simply sitting and chatting with the hostess.

Attendee Supplies

In your announcements, encourage women to bring these key items with them to their projects:

- *Trowel*
- *Gloves*
- *Sunhat*
- *Sunscreen*
- *Apron or smock*
- *Kneepads*

Publicity and Sign-Up

Create a splash for your event with excellent publicity. Be creative and create excitement—your efforts will have women running to the registration table! To provide women plenty of time to plan, begin promoting as soon as possible (eight weeks before the event). On the CD-ROM provided with this book, you'll find several publicity pieces you can use to promote your event.

On the CD-ROM, you'll find:

- Clip art

- Invitations

- Garden Group roles

Here are some ideas on how and where to publicize:

- Mail invitations to each woman in your church. (And really wow them by including a packet of seeds in the envelope.)

- Create posters using the clip art from the CD-ROM and hang them around the church (women's restrooms, bulletin boards, foyers, in the children's ministry area).

- E-mail invitations to each woman in your church. Encourage them to forward the e-mail to their friends who might be interested as well.

- Send reminder e-mails to women two weeks before the event.

- Insert an announcement in your church's newsletter or bulletin.

- Create a PowerPoint announcement using the clip art from the CD-ROM and show it before church services.

- Let your creativity shine through video commercials. Recruit women to ham it up for the camera promoting the event. Picture this: A woman is just beside herself, dramatically weeping while looking over the vast number of her dead plants, when suddenly the doorbell rings and your Garden Groups arrive! Relief and exhilaration wash over her face as she says, "Thank you, [insert church name here]. OK, so that's a silly example. Create your own, and have the women laughing all the way to the sign-up sheet.

- Ask several women to make just a few phone calls inviting women to attend, making sure that each woman of the church receives a phone call. By splitting up the list of names to call, it becomes a simple project.

- Set up a table in your church foyer with information about your event, the Garden Group roles sheet from the CD-ROM, and a sign-up sheet. You could also allow women to sign up on your church Web site.

Helpful Hint
Catch everyone's attention by attaching the customizable event invitation to a packet of seeds and inserting it into your church bulletin.

Once women begin signing up, the Publicity and Sign-Up Leader will ask women who've indicated experience in gardening to be Garden Gurus. She'll pass the names and contact information of these women to the Lead Garden Guru who will be in touch with them regarding their responsibilities. And as the day of the event nears, she'll organize women into Garden Groups. You can use garden-themed group names, such as the Gardenias, the Tulips, the Daisies, and the Orchids.

✎ Celebration Slide Show ✎

Always celebrate what women experience at your great events. In your Celebration Slide Show, you'll share the moments Reapers captured throughout the event. The Publicity and Sign-Up Leader will put your show to music, and share it at your church service the week following the event. She can also share stories from the event, which the Reapers recorded. This will not only celebrate and appreciate the women who participated…but show others what they, too, can be involved in. For the next event, they may be the first to sign up! Use the clip art provided on the CD-ROM to create slides.

Setting the Stage

From the moment women step foot into your Seeds of Friendship event, make it a refreshing, inviting experience. The main part of your event will be off-site, but don't be afraid to transform your meeting area into a garden escape! If you decide to go all out with your decorating, you might want to recruit one or two creative people to help you out.

Here are decorating ideas for each area of your space.

Entryway

Hang welcome posters and directional signs at the entrance to your event. Bring in bright balloons to cheer women as they enter. Ask your church's youth group or men's ministry to serve as greeters to open the door and direct women to the registration area.

Here's a creative way to welcome women to your event: Place "muddy" footprints on the floor, leading to the registration area. Here's how:

Make a shallow (about 2 inches deep) tub of mud by mixing dirt and water. Be sure the mixture is thick and clumpy. Outdoors, place several sheets of brown card stock as stepping-stones in front of the tub of mud. Put some boots or shoes on with a distinct sole. Step into the tub of mud, being sure the boots or shoes are well covered. Step from one sheet to the next, leaving a print on each. Allow the card stock to dry completely. Cut the footprints out of the card stock, leaving a quarter-inch border around the dried mud. Handle the dried footprints extremely carefully, so as not to disturb the dried mud. Affix each footprint to the floor with double-stick tape.

A simpler method to make muddy footprints is to cut footprints out of brown card stock. Make the same tub of mud as described above. Creatively place clumps of mud making it look realistic. Allow them to dry, cut them out, and place with double-stick tape.

Lobby

Plan for "people flow" as you choose where the registration table is set up. Decorate tables with bright tablecloths and fragrant, colorful flowers. At the registration table, you should have a sign-up sheet and multiple copies of Garden Group assignments.

Have another table with name tags and pens. Tape silk flower blossoms to the pens at this table, and then place these flower pens in a small pot or

Women will feel welcomed when they arrive and hear **The Music of the Bloomery** *CD playing softly. This garden-themed music CD is perfect as background music, or you could even lead women in singing the inspirational songs during your morning program.*

watering can. If you'll have a large number of guests, this may be another opportunity for the youth group or men's ministry to act as ushers, showing women to their tables once they have name tags.

Add fun accent props around the lobby and your meeting room: What do you think of when you envision a garden? Probably all the "extras" that go with it: a wheelbarrow (filled with potted flowers?); seed packets; watering cans; wide-brimmed straw hats; denim overalls; gardening gloves…you get the idea. Strategically place these items throughout your meeting area for fun accents.

Bathrooms

Decorate with flowerpots and lit scented candles. (It's a good idea to use candles in a glass jar, so you won't have to worry about wax dripping.)

Meeting Room

Add splashes of color throughout the room. Go for bright yellows, reds, and blues. One way to splash color into a room is by using bolts of fabric. Lengths of bright, solid colors topped with floral fabric runners add vibrancy to any surface. Also check out the inspirational Bloomery posters, shown at right, at www.groupoutlet.com. Each poster has a Scripture passage related to gardening and a gorgeous photograph of flowers. Be sure to have soft, relaxing music playing. Set up tables around the room, one per Garden Group and one for refreshments. Label each table with a specific Garden Group sign.

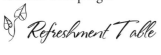

Refreshment Table

- Twinkling lights lend a festive look—consider weaving a strand or two among the items on your refreshment table.

- Present dry snacks in terra-cotta pots with small trowels for serving spoons. Or use miniature galvanized tubs and watering cans (found in the hobby section of discount stores or in craft stores) for other finger foods.

- Add warmth to the snack table by grouping votive candles in the soil-filled saucer of a large terra-cotta pot.

- Have colorful, clean gardening tools arranged around the refreshment table, adorned with bright ribbons.

Helpful Hint
For more great decorating supplies and ideas, visit www.group.com/women.

Helpful Hint

Some florists and grocery stores with floral departments are willing to donate their "day-old" flowers at the end of the day. You'd have to sort through and take out the wilted ones, but the bundles may still have many fresh and fragrant blossoms to use.

Helpful Hint

Set out sunflower seeds in a terra-cotta pot for a snack. Or make a "worms in dirt" dessert. Layer chocolate pudding in a large dish, cover it with crumbled chocolate sandwich cookies, and top with gummy worms. See the "Setting the Stage" section for more fun serving suggestions.

Centerpiece Ideas

- Plant colorful flowers in a terra-cotta pot. Invert another terra-cotta pot (of the same size). Place the pot with the flowers on top of the inverted pot, and tie a ribbon around the seam.

- Bright, single flowers in slender vases can have as much of an impact as terra-cotta pots with many blooms. For a creative touch, use old perfume bottles, wineglasses, water goblets, and salt shakers instead of vases.

- Fill empty glass jars with colorful petals. Tall and slender jars would add elegance. A local florist would be a great source for the petals. Call in advance, and let them know what you're planning. They may charge for rose petals, but may also be willing to save other petals.

- Fill a shallow terra-cotta pot with water and add a few floating candles. Sprinkle a handful of rose petals into the water.

- Borrow a desktop-size water fountain. Look for one that creates the sound of a gentle brook, and encircle the base with a garland of fresh or artificial flowers.

Refreshments and Lunch

As the women arrive at the church, the Stage Setter will provide light refreshments. There's time planned for refreshments and visiting to keep the morning relaxed and inviting. Here's a quick checklist of suggested items to have at the church:

- Plates, napkins, and utensils
- Coffee and water cups and stir sticks
- Coffee—regular and decaffeinated. Serve with sugar, sugar substitute, cream, or coffee creamer substitute.
- Hot water for tea and tea bags
- Ice water
- Fruit juice
- Pastries: muffins, bagels, or croissants
- Cheese and crackers
- Assorted fruit

You'll also want to decide what kind of a sack lunch to provide women with at the gardening site. Have at least one large water bottle per woman. The Nourisher will pick up the lunches and water for her group the morning of the event. A sample lunch menu could be: a cold sandwich, fruit, cookie, and a beverage. You could have this catered by a sandwich shop or a grocery store. Or, you can prepare the lunches yourselves. Be as simple or lavish as you'd like. The recipe below for Springtime Deli Wraps would make a great sack lunch.

Refresh Punch

This punch would be a perfect accompaniment to your refreshments in the morning.

one 12-ounce can frozen lemonade concentrate, thawed

one 12-ounce can frozen orange juice concentrate, thawed

1 cup sugar

1 teaspoon vanilla extract

1 teaspoon almond extract

7 cups cold water

4 cups cubed ice

2 liters lemon-lime soda, chilled

In a large beverage cooler, combine first six ingredients. Gently pour soda and add ice. If you wish, use limeade instead of lemonade or use a flavor-combination orange juice such as pineapple-orange-banana juice from concentrate. Serve immediately. Makes 1 gallon.

Springtime Deli Wraps

12 ounces light cream cheese spread

3 tablespoons Dijon mustard

1 ½ tablespoons honey

2 ¼ cups romaine lettuce, shredded

2 medium tomatoes, seeded and chopped

1 large green bell pepper, chopped

nine 8-inch spinach, sun-dried tomato, or whole wheat tortillas

12 ounces thinly sliced deli ham (or turkey or roast beef)

1 ¼ cups shredded Swiss cheese

9 slices bacon, crisply cooked, drained, and crumbled

Combine cream cheese, mustard, and honey in a small bowl. Shred lettuce and chop tomato and bell pepper. Spread cream cheese mixture thinly over each tortilla—within ¼ inch of the edge. Cover with ¼ cup lettuce, pressing lightly. Place two ham slices over lettuce. Sprinkle with 2 tablespoons of Swiss cheese. Sprinkle with bacon, tomato, and bell pepper. Roll each tortilla tightly. Wrap in cling wrap. Keep refrigerated. Makes 9 wraps.

Did the women in your Garden Groups form a tight bond? Encourage deepening those friendships with **Group's Dinner and a Movie: Chick Flicks.** *They'll prepare a dinner together, watch a chick flick, and discuss the spiritual themes in the movie.*

Morning Program

Your morning program will be short—just enough time to communicate what the women need to know about the day's event and to plant a few seeds of truth. The themes you touch on in your morning program will be picked up and carried by the Sowers (devotional leaders) at the project sites.

The Director will be emcee of your morning program. After women have had time to get a snack, find their Garden Group tables, and chat a little, begin your event by telling everyone just how thrilled you are they've come and how excited you are for the event. Briefly describe your morning schedule and what to expect. Describe the role of each woman in each group—everyone has an important role. The sheet with the roles will be on the tables. Have women decide at their tables who will fill each role. Once they've decided on roles, tell the Sowers to take the devotional handouts at each table with them to their project sites.

Ask women to turn to a partner at their tables and share about the greatest surprise they ever had. Give women a couple of minutes to share.

Share the Scripture theme of your event, found in Mark 4:30-32:

"Jesus said, 'How can I describe the Kingdom of God? What story should I use to illustrate it? It is like a mustard seed planted in the ground. It is the smallest of all seeds, but it becomes the largest of all garden plants; it grows long branches, and birds can make nests in its shade.' "

Ask the women to turn back to that same partner and answer this question, "How was your experience of being surprised like or unlike the mustard seed described?" Give each woman a minute to discuss.

Share this quote of Barbara Johnson's with the women, "Keep looking for the boomerang surprise in your life. Listen for the whirring sound that means it may be getting close. Always stay connected to people and seek out things that bring you joy."

Explain to women that there are surprises of joy waiting for us just around the garden hedge—just as God created the world and plants around us to be surprising and wonderful, the Kingdom of God is his *greatest* surprise. And we can begin experiencing his kingdom today, in the friendships that we sow with one another and in the kind work we do for others.

Point out a couple of the things done that morning to create surprise (see the "Splash Your Event With Surprises" section). It's small kind surprises done for others that create unexpected joy. Share that everyone can watch for ways to bring unexpected joy to others—such as serving the hostess at each location today! Encourage them to remember God, the Creator of the mustard seed, will grow us to be a beautiful part of his kingdom, surprising and blessing us (and others through us) with joy.

Before breaking to go to the hostesses' homes, pray for the women, hostesses, and the time you have together this morning. Remind the Sowers to continue your devotional throughout the day—in the car and over lunch with the devotional handouts. Encourage the journalers to write notes and stories of what women learned. Instruct the ladies on what to do after they're done with their projects and after lunch. Due to timeliness of all the groups getting back to the church at the same time, it may be of benefit to simply have the women return home when they arrive at the church.

Splash Your Event With Surprises

The tiny mustard seed becomes one of the largest plants—weave the element of surprise throughout the day of your event. Here are several ideas for you to choose from:

- Arrange valet parking the morning of the event.
- Provide a gift for each attendee at the tables (printed apron, garden shovel with a note attached, a packet of seeds, or a sunhat).
- Give each woman a mustard seed in a plastic pouch with a card

More Scripture Ideas

This event could become an annual event for your women's ministry. In years to come, replace the Scripture for the devotional with any of these Scriptures. Plan questions that spur discussion…asking how or why. Start with unique questions about their life experiences. Then, ask thoughtful questions on how this applies to the Scripture. Follow by asking questions further exploring God's truths.
Psalm 1:2-3
Isaiah 58:11
Matthew 12:33
Matthew 13:3-9
John 15:1-8
James 3:17-18

attached. "Thank you so much for coming! We're thrilled you were able to come. Please take this mustard seed and remember what God can do with the surprises and unexpected events that come into our lives." This can be waiting for women at the tables.

- Plan for the Root Team to visit the hostesses' homes while the gardening projects are going on, bringing along cookies or another fun treat.

- Ask the hostess to provide a small plant for each woman in the group as they leave her home. To not burden the hostess, the Hostess Leader could purchase the plants for all the hostesses and deliver them to the hostesses before the event.

Option to Make Your Event a Full Day

If the half-day plan is just too short for you and your ministry, extend to make it a full day. Simply use the plan outlined above and add a few items:

- Allow the Garden Gurus to plan for an afternoon of planting as well. This would provide ample time for bigger projects or a series of smaller projects.

- Provide afternoon snacks and beverages. Or, to provide another element of surprise, plan for the Root Team to visit the hostesses' homes in the afternoon with ice cream sandwiches.

- From 1:00 to 3:00 p.m. it could be pretty hot. Plan projects inside during this time, such as pruning and cleaning indoor plants, decorating containers for outdoor planting, washing windows, or doing any other little chores she might need done.

- From 3:00 p.m. to 4:30 p.m. is a better time to continue outdoor projects.

- From 4:30 to 5:00 p.m. can be spent traveling back to the church.

- Beginning at 5:15 or 5:30 p.m. would be a great opportunity for an unexpected surprise. Plan an affirmation dinner for the women. Get the men's ministry or youth ministry involved in the dinner…cooking, serving, and clean up. If your budget allows, you could have the meal professionally catered.

- After a full day of gardening, the women may not be up for a late night. Keep your evening light and simple. For example, you can show a movie or even allow the men's ministry to come up with a short "Why we appreciate you" variety show. Oh, can you imagine what they would come up with?

Port Paradise Cruise

"The Lord has told you what is good, and this is what he requires of you: to do what is right, to love mercy, and to walk humbly with your God" (Micah 6:8).

Are you ready for an island cruise?

Set sail for Port Paradise. You and your guests will have fun from beginning to end making friends, relaxing on deck, and experiencing the shore excursions.

While in Port Paradise, you'll jump ship at three ports of call: Join an energetic volleyball game or take a leisurely stroll at Good Times Bay, play in the sand at Reflection Beach, and find true treasure at Treasure Cove. And through it all, you'll meditate on God's wisdom for sailing the seas of life: "to do what is right, to love mercy, and to walk humbly with your God."

On deck, women can relax the day away at your Island Spa. And, of course, every cruise must include a bountiful buffet. We'll give you suggestions for food, decorations, and simple ideas for a little spa treatment. You can cruise on a small budget in a convenient three- to four-hour event. Warning: Your cruise will be so fun and relaxing, you may want to extend it to a full-day cruise!

Getting Started

∽ Gathering the Crew ∽

The Captain of this ship is Jesus Christ. The Crew should consist of women who are excited about serving and reaching out to other women. They should also be gifted in the area of responsibility. Spend time in prayer seeking the Captain's orders for assigning these responsibilities.

The Crew Leaders are the First Mate, Cruise Director, Shore Excursion Skipper, Master Chef, and Lead Designer.

The First Mate oversees the entire event, and may very likely be you! She will lead the Crew in planning, promoting, and implementing all aspects of the event. She will gather the supplies needed for On-Deck Activities. She should be gifted in administration and leadership.

The Cruise Director is responsible for flow of the event. As the master of ceremonies, she'll keep the event on schedule and the passengers engaged. A friendly, outgoing personality and gifts in communication and organization will set a positive tone for everyone. (See the "Step by Step Through the Cruise" section.)

The Shore Excursion Skipper is in charge of shore activities at the ports of call. She is responsible for planning, purchasing, set up, and instructions for the ports of call. She should be gifted in organization with an eye for detail. (See the "Ports of Call" section.)

The Master Chef is responsible for food and drinks. She'll work with a team to provide the bountiful buffet. She should be creative, energetic, and gifted in organization. A magnetic personality will enjoy inviting others to contribute to this fun area. (See the "Master Chef's Plan.")

The Lead Designer is responsible for creating the environment. Her team will transform the selected location into paradise. In addi-

- *Helpful Hint*
- *If you have a smaller group of*
- *women, you can combine the roles of the First Mate and the Cruise Director.*

tion to her artistic ability, she should be gifted in communication and serving. (See the "Designer Notes" section.)

Timeline

Eight weeks before your event

- Begin praying for your Port Paradise Cruise.

- Read through this chapter in its entirety.

- Recruit your Crew Leaders.

- Estimate how many women will attend your event, using figures from previous retreats or women's events as a guide. This will help you finalize location details.

Seven weeks before your event

- Meet with your Crew Leaders. (You may want Crew Leaders to read this chapter before the meeting.) At this meeting:

    - Start with prayer and decide on a purpose statement for your event.

    - Choose the event date.

    - Go over Crew Leader role descriptions and this outline of your event.

    - Decide on publicity. (See the "Publicity" section and the CD-ROM.)

    - Set a budget. Determine how much money the Lead Designer, Master Chef, and Shore Excursion Skipper have to work with.

    - Decide whether you'll charge a participant's fee.

    - Decide whether you'll provide child care.

- Reserve the area where you've decided to host the event for the day of the event and the day before for set up.

Six weeks before your event

- Launch publicity.

- Begin signing women up for your event.

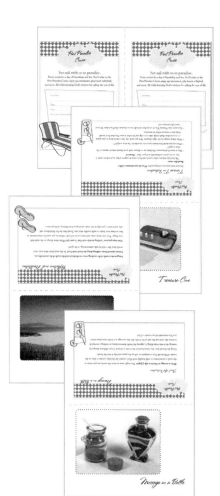

Four weeks before your event

- Continue publicity and registration.
- The Lead Designer and Master Chef gather crew members needed to help with setup and food.
- The First Mate and the Shore Excursion Skipper begin gathering supplies.

Two weeks before your event

- Continue publicity and registration.
- Request any technical support you'll need for the event.

The week of your event

- Don't forget to keep praying!
- Send an e-mail reminder to women.
- The Cruise Director reads through and prepares for the devotional.
- Confirm any food deliveries or orders.

The day before your event

- The Crew Leaders and any teams they've gathered set up and decorate the area.

The day of your event

- The Crew Leaders should arrive early to set out food and drinks, pray over the event, turn the music on, and troubleshoot any last-minute challenges.

Cruise Itinerary

- Registration and Mingling (15 to 30 minutes)
- Bon Voyage and Getting Acquainted (15 to 30 minutes)
- Setting Sail: Sailing the Seas of Life (20 to 30 minutes)
- Ports of Call and On-Deck Activities (1 to 2 hours)
- The Return Trip (15 minutes)

Let's Get Planning!

∼ Choosing a Location ∼

Consider dropping anchor someplace other than your church facilities. It's good to get away from the familiar. You can do your cruise indoors or out of doors. Some ports of call, such as Good Times Bay, are better out of doors, while relaxing on-deck may be nice indoors. The weather in your region can also determine which makes for a more pleasant event. If you live near water or a beach, that would make a perfect location, but any place can be transformed into Paradise. Is there a local, state, or federal park nearby? For smaller groups, a picnic shelter is a perfect ship deck. And many parks also have nature trails. Of course, your church may be best for your group—we just want to encourage you to consider other options.

Here's what you'll need in a location: One large area to serve as your ship deck. Women will gather here for refreshments, the devotion, and spa activities. For the devotion, you'll need seating for the ladies, and for the spa activities, you'll want to make sure it's a pleasant, relaxing, quiet place. At Good Times Bay, women will play volleyball or take a walk with a friend. Choose someplace where you can set up a volleyball net (in a gym, at a park, or on the beach) and someplace with a nature trail nearby or a sidewalk through a park. Reflection Beach will need one area where women will quietly pray and meditate on their own and one area where they'll make their Message in a Bottle crafts together (picnic tables would work well). Treasure Cove can also be set up on picnic tables or a room of tables. See the Ports of Call section and Lead Designer's Notes for more on setting up these areas.

∼ Promotion Ideas ∼

Women won't want to miss your Port Paradise Cruise. Here are some ways to get the word out.

- Word of mouth: Your volunteers are your best promoters.
- Fliers: Create fliers using the clip art from the CD-ROM and

distribute them at VBS, women's Bible studies, MOPS, preschool and other community groups where women gather. Pass out tropical fruit along with the fliers after services.

• Online: Post an announcement to your church Web site, and church related message boards. Ask anyone who has a Web site or "blog" to mention the event on her site.

• On the CD-ROM, you'll find invitations. Customize the invitations and mail them or pass them out.

• Create posters and PowerPoint announcements using the clip art on the CD-ROM.

• Perform a skit as an advertisement at your church service. Here's a script to get you started.

Promotion Skit

Jennie *is dressed for a tropical cruise (sunglasses, straw hat, flowered dress or top, large overstuffed suitcase with clothes hanging out, passport, and traveler's checks). Rushed and exhausted, she runs on stage awkwardly pulling her suitcase and trying to look through travel papers.*

Jane *is relaxed and comfortably dressed, sitting on the floor at the feet of a beach chair.*

Jane: (Puzzled) Jennie, what are you doing?

Jennie: (Excited. Doesn't wait for responses to her questions.) I heard the women at church are all going on a cruise. Oh, I have always wanted to go on a cruise. (Shows her passport to Jane.) What do you think of my passport picture? I should have worn red that day. Do you think I've forgotten to pack anything? I've got socks, suntan lotion, and traveler's checks. Do you know if the ship will cash my traveler's checks? (Waves her traveler's checks.)

Jane: Jennie, you are way too stressed out. You need a vacation for sure. But you don't need to worry about all these details. The Port Paradise Cruise is the women's Summer Wow Event. The only thing you need to do is show up at [location, date, time]. We'll relax, play volleyball, maybe have some exotic fruit, take a walk, and dip into some chocolate. You can even stop by the Island Spa for a relaxing massage. And we'll learn more about how God wants us to sail the seas of life. Here's a flier, *Martha.* If you lose this in that mess you can pick up another one at the women's ministry table.

Come on; let me help you put that stuff away.

Jennie: (As they walk off stage together) You're going to get up and help me? This is a miracle!

Master Chef's Plan

Food is the highlight of any cruise. Make it special. Will you select people to contribute, or ask everyone to bring a dish? Do you have the budget to have refreshments or a meal catered? Can you ask the men's ministry or youth ministry if a couple of volunteers would be able to serve as food hosts during the event? The Master Chef may want to recruit several women to be on her crew to help plan for food and drinks and to help set up and keep food tables neat. You can decide if you want to just stick to refreshments or serve a meal.

The time of day will determine your menu. Challenge people to bring unique fruit and tropical dishes. Here are some simple ideas: Fresh strawberries and a chocolate fountain; pound cake, angel food cake, or muffins with fresh fruit; or the always popular fruit pizza with cookie crust.

Recipes for Caribbean delights like fried plantains, bananas foster, shrimp dishes, and dishes with mangoes, papaya, and coconut can be found on Web sites such as www.recipezaar.com, www.allrecipes.com, www.cooking .com and www.foodnetwork.com. Here are a couple of very tasty dishes to get your creative juices flowing.

Calypso Cooler

One serving of this refreshing drink won't be enough. It is quick and easy to make, and even easier when you prepare it ahead of time and keep refrigerated.

lemonade flavor drink mix, dry mix for 2 quarts prepared lemonade (any variety, try raspberry lemonade for a great taste and color)

3 cups cold water

2 cups pineapple juice

1 cup cream of coconut (find this in the ethnic food isle or around the drink mixes)

Dissolve drink mix in cold water. Stir in pineapple juice and cream of coconut. Serve over crushed ice with a slice of pineapple on the glass. Serves 7.

Baked Bananas

If you are having a meal, small servings will be a nice finish. If you are having desserts only, plan on making this to serve only four. Best served hot, but still good if it's cooled.

2 tablespoons melted butter

1 tablespoon lemon juice

1 teaspoon ground cinnamon

1 teaspoon vanilla extract

4 ripe bananas

1/3 cup packed brown sugar

vanilla ice cream

Heat oven to 350 degrees. Combine first four ingredients. Quarter bananas—cut in half, then slice lengthwise. Place in baking dish with cut side up.

Coat bananas with cinnamon butter mixture using a brush, allowing mixture to seep into the bananas. Sprinkle brown sugar over bananas.

Bake uncovered at 350 degrees for 15 minutes. Serve hot over ice cream. Makes 8 small servings.

Tropical Fruit Scones

Yum! These are great right out of the oven, warmed or room temperature. You won't need to add jam or butter to these biscuits.

4 cups all purpose flour

4 teaspoons baking powder

1 teaspoon salt

4 tablespoons sugar

½ pound cold butter, cubed

1 cup tropical dried fruit

1 ½ cup buttermilk (plus a little more for tops)

sugar

Preheat oven to 400 degrees. Combine first four ingredients until well mixed. Stir in the butter until dough forms a meal like texture. Add the dried fruit. Slowly add buttermilk until dough is moist.

Separate dough into 12 large balls or 24 small balls. Place on shallow baking pan lined with parchment paper to prevent burning the bottoms. Brush dough balls with buttermilk and sprinkle with sugar. Bake 20-30 minutes for large scones. Makes 12 large scones.

- *Helpful Hint*
- *When baking scones, reduce*
- *baking temperature to 350 degrees if using a dark pan without parchment paper*

Getting the Cruise Ready to Sail

Throughout this event, women will move to different areas or stations. Some are "On-Deck" so they'll feel like they're happening on the ship. Others will be "Ports of Call" that will feel like locations women will visit off the ship. Here's what happens at each station and how to set up or prepare.

On-Deck Activities

On-deck is where women will sign in, where they'll enjoy refreshments and the devotional, and where they'll enjoy spa treatments. You'll also gather back on-deck for the return trip. At the registration table, you might want to have information on women's Bible studies or small groups available for women who are new to your ministry. The First Mate is responsible for gathering supplies needed on-deck. (A supply list follows.)

Island Spa

The word *spa* just sounds relaxing, doesn't it? Make your Island Spa as elaborate or as simple as you desire. Perhaps you have a physical therapist or professional masseuse in your group that would be willing to donate her time to give chair massages. If not, set up a few gadgets such as massage cushions, foot massagers, or hand-held massagers. If you have a water source nearby, have hand scrub and lotion available so women can give themselves hand treatments. You can also provide manicure and pedicure supplies. Or, ask nail professionals to provide manicures or pedicures during your event.

In your spa area, you may want to set up pitchers of water with glasses for women. You could also make it feel like a true island spa by having mango tea and papaya slices set out for women to enjoy. Play the island music on the CD-ROM or ocean sounds in the background to create an island ambience.

First Mate's Essential Cargo List

Here's the kit and caboodle necessary for creating your on-deck activities:

- table for registration
- name tags and markers
- buffet tables for refreshments
- table seating for refreshment time and devotional
- sound system with microphone

Island Spa

- lounge chairs
- tables for spa equipment
- massage equipment
- exfoliating scrubs and lotions
- hand towels
- manicure and pedicure supplies
- CD player with island music on the CD-ROM
- pitchers of water, mango tea, papaya slices, plates, and cups (optional)

- *Helpful Hint*
- *If women want to just hang*
- *out, laugh, and relax, set up an area on-deck to show Christian comedian videos. You can find these online and at Christian bookstores. Look for Chonda Pierce, Nicole Johnson, and Anita Renfroe. Or, show old TV shows, such as "Gilligan's Island" or "I Love Lucy." You can find TV collections at video stores and online video stores.*

Ports of Call

In this section, you'll find how to set up each port of call, and what women will do there. At each port of call, women will reflect on different parts of the theme verse for their Port Paradise Cruise. The Shore Excursion Skipper is responsible for obtaining the supplies for each port. She may want to recruit women to demonstrate the crafts at Reflection Beach and Treasure Cove. It might also be good to recruit a couple of women to keep games of volleyball going.

Treasure Cove

At this first port of call, women will consider what it means for them to "do

Supplies for Treasure Cove

- tables and chairs
- small mint tins
- decorating supplies, such as ribbons, glue, markers, package labels, card stock, stick-on gems, and stickers
- 2x3-inch slips of paper and pens
- Treasure Tin instructions from CD-ROM—simply print and make copies

- - - - - -

Supplies for Good Times Bay

- volleyball net and volleyball
- water bottles
- trail maps for the nature trail, if necessary

- - - - - -

what is right." God treasures the good things we do for him, and women will consider what it is *they're* treasuring. They'll make Treasure Tins in which they'll keep reminders of how they can "do what is right." This is a great activity to do in small groups. Women will use small mint tins, like Altoids mint tins, to create this craft. You can collect these from mint lovers ahead of time, or find them online at www.groupoutlet.com.

1. Make a Treasure Tin ahead of time to use as a sample.

2. Set up tables, and place the instructions from the CD-ROM on the table.

3. Set out tins and decorating supplies you've gathered, 2x3-inch slips of paper, and pens.

4. As women arrive at your area, instruct them to follow the instructions on the Treasure Tin instructions page.

Good Times Bay

This port of call is where women will learn to "love mercy" in their relationships with one another. Women will have the choice of a round of beach volleyball or a walk with a friend. This port will give you a bit of a breather to set up—beach volleyball requires little explanation. A sand volleyball court with a nature trail or a park with a sidewalk nearby is the ideal location for your port. A volleyball net on a lawn or in the gym of your church works, too. You may want to have several women commit to play volleyball to keep the games going. If there are no nature trails nearby, plan a walking trail through the neighborhood or around the church property—be sure to provide a simple map!

There won't be printed instructions for women at this port, but in your Bon Voyage, the Cruise Director will encourage women to think about what it means to "love mercy" while here. For those that decide to take a walk with a friend, have water bottles and trail maps available. Ask them to consider what it means to "love mercy" and how they can do this in their friendships. For those that decide to play volleyball, between rounds, have them think and discuss how they can "love mercy" in their day-to-day lives: while playing games, talking to others, going grocery shopping, and so on.

Reflection Beach

At Reflection Beach, women will take some time alone to meditate on what it means to "walk humbly with your God." This will be a quiet spot for introspection. Each woman will sit at a small "sandbox" with a sand rake, and follow the guided experience on the Reflections and Meditations Post Card.

If you'd like to add a bit of fun to Reflection Beach, have a sand castle competition. If you're not at a beach, fill several borrowed children's wading pools with sand and give teams of women one hour to create sand masterpieces.

Message in a Bottle

After women have completed the Reflections and Meditations Post Card, they'll make these sand art bottles to be a reminder to walk humbly with God.

1. Cover tables with rolled paper. Place bottles of colored craft sand on the tables, along with the other supplies. (Visit craft or hobby stores for colored sand and fun glass bottles.) Have a funnel available for each color.

2. Women will follow the instructions on the page you've printed from the CD-ROM to write a message to God on the slips of paper. They might write a commitment to walk humbly with God, a prayer for his help, a praise, or Micah 6:8.

3. They'll then use a toothpick to roll up the strip, and slip it into the bottle. Women will use the funnels to layer the colored sand in the bottles as desired. They can create different designs by turning the bottle while filling it, tapping the bottle between layers, or sticking a toothpick between the sand and the side of the bottle.

Supplies for Reflection Beach

- *Print out the Reflections Post Card (from the CD-ROM), and make copies*
- *Sand boxes. Create sandboxes by filling wide, shallow, plastic dishpans with sand. You can find the sand and dishes at a home or garden supply store.*
- *Sand rakes. You can find these at children's toy stores.*

Supplies for Message in a Bottle

- *tables and chairs*
- *colored craft sand and bottles with corks*
- *funnels*
- *toothpicks*
- *slips of paper and pens*
- *Message in a Bottle instructions from the CD-ROM*

Lead Designer Notes

The Lead Designer will transform your cruise into paradise by adding touches of decorations and ambience throughout the event. She may want to recruit another woman or two to help her brainstorm and set up. Here are great ideas for each area of your event.

Decorations On-Deck

This is where women will be hanging out, enjoying refreshments and spa treatments. Create a gangway from the registration table to the deck of the ship. This may be as simple as planks on the ground with rope handrails. You can make a banner for your cruise ship or post the promotional posters at the entrance. As women enter the ship, you could welcome each of them with flower leis.

Have the island music provided on the CD-ROM playing when women arrive. Use strings of white lights on-deck to enhance the festive mood. Add to the ambience with bamboo torches and the scent of cocoa butter candles. Have your crew wear white shirts and create the uniform look with a thin strip of black tape on top of the shoulder. If you have any ports of call volunteers, ask them to wear tropical shirts.

For easy clean up, cover all tables with roll paper. Add accents with colorful tropical fruit, confetti, decorative pieces of cloth or table runners made from colored roll paper. Floating flowers or candles are a nice touch, too.

Helpful Hint

- *Your guests can help create*
- *that island feel by coming dressed in their cruise attire—tropical shirts, swim dresses—whatever they would wear on a cruise.*

Invite a young artist to paint a mural backdrop. Allow the artist to leave business cards near her work.

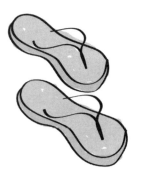

⁓ *Ports of Call Decorating* ⁓

Your First Mate will have the supplies for the activities at the ports of call. Read the Getting the Cruise Ready to Sail section for more information at what will be on-deck and at each port of call.

⚓ *Reflection Beach*

At Reflection Beach, you can set up several stations with the sand dishes on the ground for women who can sit on the ground. Include bright beach towels to sit on at each spot. Create a beach setting with colorful seashells and a fishnet on the tables. A beach chair and umbrella are easy decorations. For an added touch, spread inexpensive sand over black landscaping cover. Make the area just big enough for the beach towel and umbrella. Have a couple of beach balls lying about. If you're at a beach, you and your crew could make simple sand castles the morning of the event surrounding the area.

⚓ *Treasure Cove*

Go for a pirate's feel at this location. In the center of the tables, pile fake strands of pearls and gems. Or, find an inexpensive treasure chest at a craft store, and fill it with fake gems and pearls hanging over the edge. You could put the CD-ROM instructions in this chest. Add some greenery such as large potted plants or decorative palm trees to this area, available at party supply stores.

⚓ *Good Times Bay*

No decorations are necessary at this area, but you could enliven it with bamboo torches and beach balls around the volleyball court. (But not close enough to get in the way!)

- *Helpful Hint*
- *Ask your children's minister*
- *director if there are decora-*
  tions from previous years' VBS
  programs available. And for
  more decorating ideas, visit
  www.group.com/women.

Step by Step Through the Cruise

Read through this section to familiarize yourself with the flow of events and for the scripts for your devotional times.

Registration and Mingling

Make a name tag for each guest while she signs in. Crew should act as greeters and mingle with passengers, inviting them to fill a plate and have a seat.

Bon Voyage and Getting Acquainted

The Cruise Director will be the master of ceremonies. Once women have settled in at tables and gotten to meet their neighbors, say:

Welcome aboard the Port Paradise Cruise. I'll be your Cruise Director, and I'm here to make sure you have a relaxing and fun time. We have a short sail to Port Paradise where you will have a variety of ports of call to enjoy.

First let's take some time to get to know each other. I'm sure we have women from all over on this cruise. At your tables, tell one another your names and where you were born. Figure out who was born the farthest away.

Give women a few minutes to chat. (You may want to ask the woman who was born farthest away at each table to stand, and find out who was born the farthest away of all your guests.) Then say: **OK, now go around the table and tell one another how many places you've lived.** Pause. (You may want to have the women who have lived the most or fewest places stand again, to see who the "winners" are.)

Now take one minute each to describe your favorite getaway to those

at your table—is it an island cruise? A European tour? A backwoods campsite? Allow about 10 minutes.

Now that we know each other a little better, let's ask God to bless our event and draw us closer to him.

Open your event with prayer and ask that women would grow closer to one another and to him.

Setting Sail: Sailing the Seas of Life

SAY: **Today we're going to enjoy a day in paradise, and we're also going to consider God's wisdom for how to sail the seas of life. Sometimes navigating through life can seem as confusing as figuring out a pirate's treasure map, with stains on the map, pieces missing, and trails that seem to lead nowhere. Luckily God has given us a clear map for navigating the seas of life. Let's read our theme verse for the Port Paradise Cruise:**

"The Lord has told you what is good, and this is what he requires of you: to do what is right, to love mercy, and to walk humbly with your God" (Micah 6:8).

Well, that doesn't seem so complicated! God has given us three things in that verse that are vital as we sail the seas of life: to do what is right, to love mercy, and to walk humbly with our God. Turn to a partner at your table and discuss what it means to "do what is right." Is it helping the poor? Is it loving your family? Give one or two examples of what doing right should look like in your life. You'll have just two minutes! Pause.

The second navigational cue God gives us is to "love mercy." To be merciful means to be compassionate, kind, and forgiving. Turn to your partner and tell one another about a time someone was merciful to you and how it affected you. You'll have just one minute each. Pause. **Now take a minute to tell your partner how your own actions would change if you loved mercy at all times.** Pause.

The last direction from God is to "walk humbly with your God." Isn't it comforting to know that as we navigate through life, God is there walking right beside us? He doesn't ask us to do right and act merciful without his help—we can do it because we're humbly walking with him.

Perhaps you're even out on a stormy sea right now and can't see anything but the waves mounting up around you. Close your eyes right now and picture yourselves out on the sea that represents your life. What are you doing? Are you in the middle of a storm? Is it clear sailing? Are you

playing in the surf? Pause. **Now picture God walking beside you. How does the knowledge that God is right there wherever you are on the seas make you feel? Joyful? Relieved? Scared?**

Keep your eyes closed and pray a prayer to God. Perhaps you want to thank him for the smooth seas in your life and his presence in them. Perhaps you want to take his hand and ask for his guidance on a stormy sea. Whatever it is, take a minute now to talk to God.

Pause, and then finish: **Dear God, thank you for giving us a compass to navigate through the seas with. Thank you for walking right beside us every step. We ask you to bless today as we are refreshed in our friendships and as we meditate more on what your direction to us means.**

Now take some time to tell women about each area you've set up: the on-deck activities including the Island Spa, Reflection Beach, Good Times Bay, and Treasure Cove. Tell them how long they'll have for all of the activities and any other directions they'll need. You may want to have the Shore Excursion Skipper give brief descriptions of each port of call here.

As there are no instructions at the Good Times Bay, make sure women know what activities are available. Also encourage them to discuss what it means to love mercy between volleyball games. They can discuss what it means while playing games and in day-to-day life. Encourage women to find a new friend to take a stroll at Good Times Bay if you have a nature trail nearby. This will be a great opportunity to discuss how they can "love mercy" in their friendships. Then say:

Each of our ports will continue our exploration of what God's direction in Micah 6:8 means in our lives. Our journey today will take us to some areas of our lives that may be unexplored. I encourage you to do what you enjoy but also to step out of your comfort zone. You may discover hidden treasures or a breathtaking view that could change your life. Enjoy your visit to Paradise.

Ports of Call and On-Deck Activities

Dismiss the women to enjoy all the activities you've set up. Give the women a specific time to return to the ship deck. Have your crew and volunteers available at each port and on deck to make sure women know what to do and are having a good time. After the allotted time elapses, have the crew gather women back together on deck.

The Return Trip

Have a brief time together after the women have enjoyed a fun day in Port Paradise to close your time in prayer.

ASK: **Did you have fun today? Turn to a partner and tell them your favorite thing you did today.** Pause.

I hope that you had a great time relaxing with friends and exploring God's truth. Turn to a partner again and tell one another one thing that you learned or that you want to put in action regarding our theme verse. Maybe there's some good out there that you feel you should do. Perhaps there's a person you need to be more merciful toward. Perhaps you need to be more aware of walking with God each day. Tell your partner about it now. You'll have a total of four minutes. Pause.

I encourage you to make a commitment to take an action step toward what you just shared with your partner. Take a moment with me now to pray silently to God about it. I'll close the prayer after a minute or two. Pause.

Lord, we want you to be the Captain and Director of our lives. Help us to walk humbly with you each day and remember your presence right next to us. As we walk with you, we want to follow you in doing right and showing mercy to those around us. Help us remember each day the paradise with you that you've promised us. In Jesus' name, amen.

Thank your guests for coming, and tell about upcoming Bible studies or small group opportunities or plans for the next women's event. Encourage the women to talk to designated crew members about these opportunities or pray with them about disputes they need to settle in their lives.

Encourage the women to stay around and visit. Many will help clean up as they see the Crew working. Have your most visible leaders mingle without looking too busy to talk. Be sure to look for those quiet first timers that don't know anyone. Introduce them to a group of outgoing minglers.

Follow-Up

Gather all available crew after the guests have gone. Spend time praising God for the seen and unseen work he did through this event. Get feedback from the crew. Here are some questions to ask:

- What went over well? Why?

- What would you do differently for the next event?

• Did anyone share an "ah-ha" moment with you? (Share only appropriate observations and conversations.)

• What follow up contacts or activities came to light during this event? Is there someone who needs an invitation to lunch? Designate someone to follow up as needed.

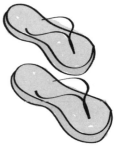

Culinary Queens

"A woman who fears the Lord will be greatly praised. Reward her for all she has done. Let her deeds publicly declare her praise" (Proverbs 31:31).

Get ready for an experience with friends you'll never forget. Do you love to cook? Hate to cook? Or are you so confused about it all you have no idea where to start? Why not spend a day with friends, old and new and learn how to turn your kitchen and cooking into something you may have never expected. You'll experience great food, fashion, fun, and friendship.

Remember the days as a young girl when you would sit up all night with girlfriends, laughing and talking? Now that we're all grown, those friendships and those times of laughter become more and more rare. So how do we bring a group of individual and unique women together to bond and grow deep in friendships? What is a bond every woman shares? Not every woman is married; not everyone has kids; not all have careers. But we all eat! *Food is our bond!* We all have a relationship with food. Some love it; some hate it; some are scared by it. However you may feel toward it, we can use it to pull us all together.

Fall is the time of harvest, of bringing in our bounty (from the grocery store or from the garden) and preparing to use it in the coming months that will hold so many celebrations. Fall is the perfect time of year to get excited about what's just around the corner, to get our kitchens and our recipes in order.

And even if not everyone is a Culinary Queen yet, every woman will have a ball at this event. Women will create their very own Kitchen Couture. What is Kitchen Couture? It's an apron of course! But not just any old apron. It's definitely *not* your grandmother's apron. Each woman will decorate one and put a little bit of herself into it, telling her story. Then she'll strut it on the Culinary Queens runway! Women will also build up their recipe books with one another's favorite recipes. And they'll contemplate what it looks like to be God's kind of women by looking at Proverbs 31.

Your Culinary Queens experience will change the way women view not only their kitchens but also themselves. So, grab a girlfriend, your favorite recipe, and your imagination and let's have some fun, Culinary Queen style, that is!

Getting Started

∽ The Royal Court ∽

What you need first is a Royal Court—all the women who are going to help you pull this off. You need a great team to have a great event! The jobs that need to be filled by your Royal Court are:

The Event Empress: This woman will know all the details of the event and will keep her court informed and equipped. She's the go-to girl! She'll be the one listed in your church bulletin or program as the questions start coming in about your exciting event. She'll also recruit greeters for the day of the event. (She should read this chapter in its entirety. See the Greeting and Check-In section for more on greeters.)

The Promoting Princess: This woman will be in charge of getting women excited for your event through promoting away. She'll find publicity materials on the CD-ROM. She'll recruit a team to lead registration and ticket sales for the event. This team will also be in charge of check-in the day of the event. (See the Promotion section and the Greeting and Check-In section.)

The Design Duchess: This member of your court will create an exciting, fun atmosphere for your event through all the senses. She'll want to recruit a team to help her out with planning and set up. She and her team will be responsible for buying, borrowing, and rounding up all decorations. (See the Decorating section.)

The Countess of Tech: You'll need technical support in some capacity. If you're doing a small event, you'll still need microphones and a music player. If you're doing a larger event, you'll need a soundboard, a PowerPoint with words to any worship songs you use, lighting, maybe even fog machines for your fashion show! This woman will be in charge of all the details and will recruit a team if necessary.

The Baroness of Ceremonies: (Otherwise known as the master of ceremonies!) Find that lady who has no fear of public speaking. She should make your group laugh and make them think. She'll set the tone for your entire evening. An emcee is very important for a great women's event. Choose this person carefully. She can be the difference between a good event and a great one. (See the Step-by-Step Through the Event section.)

The Drama Queen: This woman will form a team to break the ice with hilarious dramas. She needs to be energetic and have no fear of hamming it up. (See the Promotion section and the Drama section.)

The Couture Craft Ruler: This woman will be in charge of buying all the supplies necessary for the Kitchen Couture Aprons and Cookbooks.

The Refreshment Regent: Here we are with food again! This woman will be in charge of the refreshments at your event and will recruit a team of women to help her plan. (See the Refreshments section.)

Timeline

Ten weeks before your event

- Begin praying for your event.
- Read through this chapter in its entirety.
- Develop a Royal Court.
- Set the budget.
- Estimate how many women will attend your event, using figures from previous events as a guide. This will help you determine cost, supplies, and meeting room needs.

Nine weeks before your event

- Have a first meeting with your Royal Court. At this meeting, cover these bases:
  - Go over role descriptions and this outline of events.
  - Select when and where to host your event.
  - Decide on publicity.
  - Decide whether you'll charge a participant's fee.

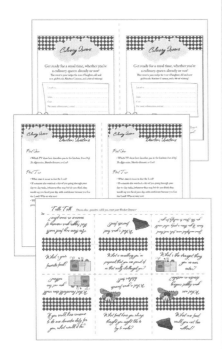

Helpful Hint

Do your best to have your final count for your event at least two weeks ahead of the event. This will allow you to purchase the correct amount of supplies. Also, if you are having anything printed or shipped, there will be enough of a cushion to have adequate time for delivery.

- Decide whether you'll provide child care.
- Decide on what kind of refreshments you'll have—a brunch, hors d'oeuvres, or a potluck, perhaps?
- Reserve the area where you'll host your event.

Eight weeks before the event

- Launch publicity.
- The Royal Court recruits teams as necessary.

Six weeks before the event

- Begin event registration.
- Don't forget to keep praying!
- The Couture Craft Ruler begins scouting and purchasing supplies.

Four weeks before the event

- Continue publicity and registration.
- The Baroness of Ceremonies prepares for the program.
- The Decorating Duchess plans and gathers supplies for decorating.
- The Refreshment Regent finalizes food plans.
- The Drama Queen and her team plan and rehearse.
- The Countess of Tech plans for technical needs and reserves equipment necessary.

Two weeks before the event

- Mail or e-mail reminders to registered participants.
- Purchase event supplies

The day before your event

- The Event Empress prints out the Devotion Questions card and the Table Talk cards to put at each table.
- The Royal Court decorates and sets up craft and food areas.

The Day of your event

6:00 p.m. . . . . . . Women arrive and check-in

6:00 to 6:15 . . . . Women will indulge in refreshments and mingle at their tables

6:15 to 6:45 . . . . Welcome and Drama
6:45 to 7:30 . . . . Kitchen Couture and Table Talk
7:30 to 7:45 . . . . Kitchen Couture Fashion Show
7:45 to 8:00 . . . . Closing

*Arrange this schedule to your needs. You can also make this a day or morning event.

Two weeks after your event

• Hold a Royal Court Reception to thank your helpers.

Who Should Come?

This event is set up to be a time when all the women of your church can come together and hopefully bring a few girlfriends with them, too. This is a fun time to invite friends to church without being too "churchy." Encourage the women of your group to invite a girlfriend who doesn't go to your church, maybe one who doesn't go to church at all. How about the neighbor across the street? The women you chat with each morning at the coffee pot? What about one of the moms from your child's sports team? How about the mom of one of your child's classmates? The lady who kicks away at Tae Bo with you each morning?

Moms, how about your junior high or high school aged daughters? This is a great mother/daughter event for you to host. It can also be something special to do for the young women of your church. (You'll help them build a recipe book as you build your own!)

Promoting

Start your promoting several months out to allow yourself the time to do this event right. When you promote, you'll want to make sure to tell women to each bring her favorite recipe to share on a 5x7-inch index card. Ask each

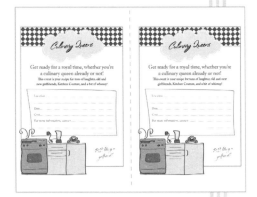

to include with the recipe a short note about it. Is it a holiday tradition? Does it have a special significance? Where did they get the recipe? This'll get women bonding from the get-go.

Here are several ways to promote for your event:

- Customize and print out the invitations from the CD-ROM and mail them to each woman in your church. (Everyone loves to get mail!)

- Create posters using the clip art from the CD-ROM and hang them around the church (women's restrooms, bulletin boards, foyers, in the children's ministry area).

- Create refrigerator magnets using the clip art from the CD-ROM and self-adhesive magnet tape to pass out at church. Women will see the reminder of your event each time they go for a snack.

- Give each woman who registers for the event a ticket to present at the door. This will make her feel like she's going someplace special! Use the clip art on the CD-ROM to create tickets.

- E-mail invitations to each woman in your church. Encourage them to forward the e-mail to their friends who might be interested as well.

- Send reminder e-mails to women two weeks before the event.

- Insert an announcement in your church's newsletter or bulletin using the clip art on the CD-ROM.

- Create a PowerPoint announcement using the clip art from the CD-ROM and show it before church services.

- Recruit your Drama Queen and her team to do a skit as an announcement during church services.

- Set up a registration table at church, hosted by Culinary Queens in full royal attire: tiaras, boas, and aprons. It'll draw women to the registration table.

Decorating and Design

The Design Duchess will add some royal oomph to your event with fun decorating touches. Your efforts will be the ladies' first impression—so make it big! Start with your Royal Court. Encourage them to come dressed in loud aprons, chef's hats, crowns, royal robes, and so on. Their fun attire will get the energy going for a lively night.

For your decorating touches, think queenly. You can use feather boas to decorate your buffet tables. Attach candy rings to napkin rings. Use white twinkle-lights to line your stage or runway. Pick one or two colors to carry throughout all your decorations to make the biggest impact; purple would be fitting for a royal theme.

Next, consider your entrance. Think red carpet for your royalty (or rolled paper if that's your budget). How about having a court jester as you approach your culinary castle? Recruit the youth group to serve as jesters in the entrance and foyer. (If they have juggling skills, even better!)

In your main meeting room, most tables can hold eight to ten women. Try not to have more at a table than eight so everyone can see the stage. If you can, have just five or six women to a table—it's a much less intimidating number to share with. There also needs to be enough room for workspace on the table for their crafts, so keep that in mind when decorating the tables.

If holding a larger event, you may want to consider turning all but one of your restrooms into women's restrooms for the day. Cover the men's signs with women's signs. You'll want to post a sign stating where the available men's restroom will be.

As far as the room layout, you'll need a stage, and a runway. Set tables and possibly ironing boards with irons around the perimeter of the room to use during the crafts. Your food tables should be set up outside of that room if at all possible. This allows any clean up to take place without distracting from the event.

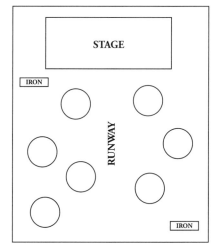

Drama

The Drama Queen and her team are a big part of making your event a hit. They can make up fun dramas to perform at church services or make a video commercial to promote your event beforehand. You could perform a short teaser fashion show using the music from the CD-ROM to get the ladies intrigued. You can also do an extreme makeover show, in which a hopeless, frazzled woman dreading the kitchen and all that it holds is turned from a Cinderella type character into a beautiful culinary queen.

The drama team will also perform "The Perfect Woman Drama," which will need four performers. See the Perfect Woman Drama section. The drama team can also be a key part of the Kitchen Couture Fashion Show. Let their enthusiasm be contagious, and let them lead the women in getting the nerve up to strut on the catwalk.

Refreshments

The Refreshment Regent will plan all the tasty tidbits for the event. Decide what scale you want your food to be on. You can do dessert, brunch, or appetizers. If you have the budget, hire a caterer to make the event extra special for women. Or, if your facility has a kitchen, the refreshments team can have its own mini potluck, each bringing her favorite dessert or appetizer.

Each woman will be asked to bring her favorite recipes to create a cookbook, so you could also ask them to bring the dish prepared. Keep in mind women's schedules when asking to bring a dish. If your crowd will be primarily busy career women, asking them to bring a dish may be an added stress to what should be a fun event. Also, consider finances for the women in your church. If bringing food would be a financial burden to them, please be aware of that as well. The last thing you want to do is have the ladies perceive this as a burden, or one more thing for them to get done on their to-do list. Maybe you just want to bless your ladies with some beautiful scrumptious food available for them. The beauty of this event is it can fit any size women's group and any budget for your ministry event.

Whatever you provide, make sure to also have water and a beverage available, such as coffee or iced tea. Here are some crowd-pleasing recipes to use at your event:

Decadent Mud Balls

8 ounces cream cheese

1 package chocolate sandwich cookies

one 20-ounce package white almond bark

food coloring (optional)

10-ounces chocolate bark (half a package)

Process cookies in a food processor, and pulse in cream cheese. Roll into 1/2-inch balls. Melt the white almond bark, and dip balls into it. (You can color the almond bark if you wish with food coloring.)

Melt the chocolate bark, and drizzle it over the balls. Cool and store in refrigerator once set. Makes approximately 2 dozen balls.

Miss Alice's Gingersnaps

1 ½ cup margarine or butter

2 eggs

½ cup molasses

2 cups sugar, plus sugar for dipping

2 teaspoons cinnamon

4 teaspoons baking soda

4 ¼ cups flour

1 ½ tablespoons powdered ginger

2 teaspoons ground cloves

Cream all wet ingredients in a large bowl. Gradually blend in sifted dry ingredients. Chill dough for 1 to 2 hours, until cooled and firm. Form into 1-inch balls. Roll the balls in sugar. Bake in preheated oven at 350 degrees for 10 minutes. Be careful not to over cook. Makes 2 dozen cookies.

Table Hostesses

A key part to making your event a success is making each woman feel involved and valued. Do this with a hostess at each table. This woman will lead the discussion questions, making sure everyone gets a chance to talk. She'll ensure everyone is connecting and laughing.

You don't have to arrange for hostesses ahead of time—just have some indication at one of the place settings of who will be the hostess. It may be a tiara on her plate (which we think is the most fun idea!), a gaudy bead necklace, or a candy-ring used as a napkin ring. During your event, simply indicate that the person with this item will be the hostess for that table, and she'll need to make sure everyone gets a chance to talk during discussions.

So are you ready to get down to business and read about all the fun activities you'll host? Read on!

Step by Step Through the Event

∽ Greeting and Check-In ∽

Begin your event with a bang by having greeters. (The Event Empress should recruit these women.) Have women outside the building greeting women and have some in the lobby. They should be dressed in tiaras and decorated aprons. They can also wear their hair in up-dos and have rings on every finger for some extra dazzle. The aprons will give the women attending a hint of what they'll be doing and inspire them for when they make their own aprons. Have these women play up the royal theme, jovially greeting newcomers. If the greeters are bold, they could even use their best British accents, drawling, "Welcome dahlings!"

Inside the doors, have women collect tickets to create a grand sense of ceremony. You'll also know how many women were at your event, which will help with planning future events. Even if your event is done at no charge as a ministry outreach, your tickets help the women feel a part of something special. You can create tickets using the clip art from the CD-ROM.

If you're looking to grow your women's ministry, have a two-part ticket. Have the price of your event cover two women, and the tickets can be buy one—get one free. You'll be amazed at the turnout of women for your event. (Everyone loves a bargain!) For example, if you need to make $5 per woman to cover the cost of the event, sell "BOGO" tickets for $10. No woman will want to waste a perfectly good ticket—they *will* find someone to bring! Just make sure you have people sign up at the ticket table to let you know the number of people coming with their ticket, so you know the number attending for proper ordering of all materials needed. Have a list of women who registered at check-in in case women forget their tickets.

Have the ticket-takers direct women to tables to make themselves name tags and to drop off the recipes they brought. Set up a large stock pot for the recipes women have brought to be placed in. Let them know that they can get themselves some treats from the refreshment table and then find a seat and chat.

Helpful Hint

The greeters can have their own pre-event apron decorating session to prepare. The aprons should represent their personal style: maybe hand painted country themes; or feather boas, rhinestones and bling glued on; or Scripture verses and floral. See the Kitchen Couture section for more ideas.

ᴄ♥ *Welcome* ♥ᴄ

The Baroness of Ceremonies will be the hostess with the mostest and will get your party rolling. First open the event with a prayer. Thank God for each woman who came and pray that God would draw them closer to him as they enjoy one another.

She can begin the event by saying something like: **Welcome to our first annual Culinary Queens Gala! OK, you might not feel like a Culinary Queen yet, but our hope is that you leave here having found a little bit of one already inside of you. Today, we're going to help you tackle your home, apartment, townhouse, or condo with confidence and style! No matter what your stage of life, if you love to cook, hate to cook, or just don't know the first thing about cooking, everyone will leave feeling like they have one more tool to tackle life. You'll leave with a new collection of recipes, you'll have an apron that will help you feel and look great, and, most importantly, you'll find out that the everyday grind of life doesn't have to be something we dread. God has fully prepared us to be the best women we can be! Hopefully, among the laughter today, you might learn something new about a friend and maybe even yourself!**

God has made each of us unique. Not only are we unique, but we are all beautifully and wonderfully made. Psalm 139:14 says, "Thank you for making me so wonderfully complex! Your workmanship is marvelous—how well I know it." That's it right there ladies—we are all marvelously complex. You may not yet realize there is a domestic diva hidden inside of you, but every woman here has gifts that God has given her. Maybe you feel like your only gift in the kitchen is that you can open the pickle jar, maybe you prefer eating to cooking, or maybe you think you can give Martha Stewart a run for her money.

Have women discuss the following question with partners or with their tables. This question appears on the Devotion Question cards you've printed out and set at each table. (Update this question with more current shows as necessary.)

> • Which TV show best describes you in the kitchen: *Iron Chef, The Apprentice, Martha Stewart,* or *Lost*?

SAY: **No matter where your skills lie, God has made each of us special. We each bring unique talents to the table. Sometimes in our busy world, it's easy to not feel quite so special. But here today, we're recognizing that each of you is a queen in her own way.**

> *Helpful Hint*
> *If you'd like, have the women sing some upbeat worship songs to set the tone for your night—you're there to praise God and have fun!*

Our Drama Queen and her ladies in waiting have prepared a little skit for us that will remind us of the pressure we sometimes feel when faced with all the tasks that face us each day.

The Perfect Woman Drama

The Drama Queen and her team will perform this fun skit for the ladies. Here are the parts:
- Narrator 1
- Narrator 2
- Proverbs 31 actress
- 21st-century actress

Have the narrators use lots of inflection in their voices, and ask the two actresses to use great dramatic flair. You can use props, or have the women mime. If you have props, have them ready for the women on the stage on two small tables. Photocopy the following skit for your drama team:

The Drama Queen: Do you ever feel like there's just too much to do? That once you have one thing done, another thing equally important pops up? And another, and another? What would the perfect woman look like? In Proverbs 31 in the Bible, we get a glimpse of what that looked like in ancient times. It says she is worth more than precious rubies. Who doesn't like rubies? Let's find out what the 21st-century Proverbs 31 woman looks like.

Narrator 1: Who can find a virtuous and capable wife? She is more precious than rubies. Her husband can trust her, and she will greatly enrich his life. She brings him good, not harm, all the days of her life. She finds wool and flax and busily spins it.

(Enter Proverbs 31 woman, dressed modestly in a Bible-times robe, busily crocheting something.)

Narrator 2: The 21st-century woman eats flax seeds on her omega-3 rich Weight Watcher's diet, and runs to the gym to her spin class.

(Enter 21st-century woman, clad in workout gear (as outrageous as you wish), carrying a workout mat and looking at a food pyramid guide.)

Narrator 1: She is like a merchant's ship, bringing her food from afar. She gets up before dawn to prepare breakfast for her household and plan the day's work for her servant girls.

(She picks up and inspects some fruit from a basket and begins to chop it.)

Narrator 2: She knows her ice cream man by name as he brings her ice cream and bread sticks from his truck. She gets up before dawn to prepare

Eggos and Pop Tarts, and takes her turn in the neighborhood carpool.

(She sets down her mat and pyramid guide and picks up and looks at some frozen food boxes.)

Narrator 1: She goes to inspect a field and buys it; with her earnings she plants a vineyard.

(She squats and inspects some dirt on the ground, running it through her fingers.)

Narrator 2: She dabbles in real estate and has become a gold star eBay power seller.

(She types into her laptop and cheers and throws her fist in the air saying, "I got it!")

Narrator 1: She is energetic and strong, a hard worker. She makes sure her dealings are profitable; her lamp burns late into the night.

(She lights an oil lamp.)

Narrator 2: She is energetic and headstrong, a good multi-tasker. She shops the clearance racks; her aromatherapy candles burn late into the night.

(She lights an aromatherapy candle.)

Narrator 1: Her hands are busy spinning thread, her fingers twisting fiber.

(She picks back up her crocheting and works away.)

Narrator 2: Her hands are busy typing on her Blackberry, and her fingers fly as she plays an Xbox game with her son.

(She picks up a game control and wildly pretends to be pushing buttons, leaning with the motions.)

Narrator 1: She extends a helping hand to the poor and opens her arms to the needy.

(She mimics bending down to hug a child.)

Narrator 2: She sends emergency aid to floods and tsunamis, and volunteers at the soup kitchen.

(She pulls out her checkbook and begins writing a check.)

Narrator 1: She has no fear of winter for her household, for everyone has warm clothes. She makes her own bedspreads. She dresses in fine linen and purple gowns.

(She picks up a deep purple robe or swath of cloth and begins to measure it.)

Narrator 2: She has no fear of winter for her household because all of them have sleepers from L.L. Bean. She dresses like royalty in her rhinestone-studded jeans from The Gap.

(She picks up and appreciates some flashy jeans, holding them up to her figure.)

Narrator 1: Her husband is well known at the city gates, where he sits with the other civic leaders. She makes belted linen garments and sashes to sell to the merchants. She is clothed with strength and dignity, and she laughs without fear of the future.
(She busily looks through her piles of cloth and crocheting, smiling to herself.)

Narrator 2: Her husband is well known, for he sits in the airport with the other frequent flyers; the pharmaceutical reps, business men, and commodities buyers. She sells Pampered Chef and hosts Mary Kay parties, too. She is clothed with strength from doing Pilates, and she laughs with no laugh lines thanks to Botox.
(She unrolls the workout mat and starts doing stretches or push-ups.)

Narrator 1: When she speaks, her words are wise, and she gives instructions with kindness. She carefully watches everything in her household and suffers nothing from laziness. Her children stand and bless her. Her husband praises her:
(She continues working busily at her pile of cloth, with a kind look on her face.)

Narrator 2: When she speaks, she is wise, and she gives detailed instructions for the sitter. She carefully TiVo's all that is watched in her house. Her children stand as tall as her. Her husband always e-mails her.
(She gets untangled from her workout and stands.)

Narrator 1: "There are many virtuous and capable women in the world, but you surpass them all!" Charm is deceptive, and beauty does not last; but a woman who fears the Lord will be greatly praised. Reward her for all she has done. Let her deeds publicly declare her praise.

Narrator 2: There are many virtuous and capable women in the world, but these days, it's hard to do it all. Charm is deceptive, and beauty lasts a little longer these days; but a woman who fears the Lord will be greatly praised. Send her to a spa for all she has done. Let all her deeds become public in her blog and web page.

The Drama Queen: Let's praise these women for all they've done. *(Lead the audience in cheering for the drama team as they take a bow.)*

After the skit, the Drama Queen should discuss it with the women, saying:

Wow! I don't know about you, but I get tired just watching that! All the things on our plate can seem overwhelming. But the Proverbs 31 woman didn't see her tasks as drudgery or get overwhelmed, but took pride and satisfaction in her work. Was she a super-woman or how did she handle all that was on her plate? Let's read that last line again. "Charm is deceptive, and beauty does not last; but a woman who fears the Lord will be greatly praised."

So her wit wasn't her secret. And her great looks weren't what got her by. What was it? She feared the Lord. And the secret to being successful in the 21st-century is the same. It's not our laptop, our Pampered Chef tools, or our business degree that'll get us by. We can face life with confidence and a smile because we fear the Lord.

Have women discuss the next three questions on the Devotion Questions cards at their table:

- What does it mean to fear the Lord?

- If someone else watched a skit of you going through your day-to-day tasks, (whatever they may be) do you think they would say you faced your day with confidence because you fear the Lord? Why or why not?

- What can you do to have this daily fear of the Lord while going about the day's tasks?

Call women back together and say: **God has given us what we need to succeed in life. Being a Proverbs 31 woman isn't an unattainable goal that only super women can reach. No matter how hectic our days are or how unskilled we feel, all we really need is to fear and trust in the Lord. If we entrust our days to him, he will help us and guide us through them. Let's pray now, asking God to help us to fear him each day and be the women he desires us to be.** Lead women in praying.

SAY: **So, if you are one of the women who dreads domestication, let's turn it from drudgery into a delight with our Kitchen Couture!**

⌒ *Kitchen Couture* ⌒

The Baroness of Ceremonies should direct women about how to go about making their Kitchen Couture. The tables will need to be cleared of any plates or other items from the refreshments so women can work at the tables. Let women know where to pick up the blank aprons and what decorating supplies are available.

Helpful Hint

We have fun decorating and gift ideas for you, such as pewter charms to give as a gift to each culinary queen, at www.group.com/women.

Empty any water out of the irons ahead of time as any amount of water will ruin an appliqué.

Helpful Hint

Coo-what? **Couture** *refers to new women's fashions, and is pronounced koo-toor. (Well, kind of. If you've studied French, you can do a more sophisticated version,* **koo-tür.***)*

Tell them that the idea of the aprons is to make them represent themselves. They could tell a story about them, reflect a hobby or interest, or show their personality. Above all, they should be fun. The point is to look good, no, *beautiful*, even in the kitchen. It's easy to get discouraged about household chores, even to resent the tasks outlined in Proverbs 31. But when they put on their Kitchen Couture at home, they won't be able to help but smile and remember that they're Culinary Queens.

Around the perimeter of the room, have tables set up holding all of your decorating supplies and treasures. The more you can have to decorate with the better. Remember, each woman is unique so the aprons will come out in every style from country to funky, to bling-bling and everything in between. Look for craft supplies at craft stores and dollar stores. Some ideas for your decorating supplies to have on hand are: fabric paints, puff paints, glitter paints, fabric markers and pens, stencils, appliqués, iron-on transfers, beads and sequins, pearls, feather boas, loose feathers, fabric glue, and more fabric glue, fabric scraps, and anything you can think of to put on those aprons!

You can even charge a couple extra dollars for ladies that want a digital photo taken of themselves with their girlfriends. This can be printed on-site from any ink jet printer on to iron-on transfer sheets that are available at most office supply stores. These can then be ironed on to their aprons and embellished. This becomes more than an apron, more than a souvenir from a retreat, but a personal scrapbook of the fun they had with their girlfriends. If doing any type of iron-on, make sure you ask every woman possible on your team to bring an ironing board and their iron from home to be used for the event. (And be sure you have adequate electrical outlets, too!)

Give women about 30 minutes to create their Kitchen Couture. While decorating, the table hostess will lead the women in the discussion questions on the table. See the Table Talk section for more on this.

Couture Cookbooks

Another option to do along side the aprons is a Couture Cookbook.

Women will each get a white 3-ring binder and decorate them with the apron decorating supplies. They'll put all the recipes women brought in this binder and take this home.

You can have several volunteers on hand (preferably not women from your event, perhaps members of the youth group or men's group) to make copies of the recipes women brought. Once everyone has arrived, this team will step into high gear and make a copy of every recipe for each woman, organize the recipes into stacks, and hole punch them. The number of people you'll need to make copies will depend on the number of copy machines you have available and how many women are attending.

However, if your church only has one copier, the obvious choice would be to collect the recipes and print them off after the event, and then women can put them into the binder that they decorated at your event. In this case, women can pick the recipes up at church or, if your budget allows, you can mail every attendee a packet with all the new recipes.

Either way, you can also include in this packet a flyer for your Women's Ministry program, an event calendar, service times, and a letter thanking the ladies for coming and taking time out of their schedules.

If you can have the copies of the recipes made fast enough, women can insert the recipes themselves after decorating their cookbooks. It's a good idea to have several sample cookbooks decorated and sitting around to inspire the ladies.

Table Talk

While decorating and assembling their cookbooks and aprons, the table hostesses will ask a few questions from the cards that will be located on each table. Print these cards from the CD-ROM. Have a short open microphone time with a couple of brave volunteers to share their biggest cooking or home disaster stories (admit it, everyone has at least one). Be prepared to share one first to get the ball rolling.

Again, during decorating you want your women to not only be working on their projects, but to be talking and building relationships at the same time. Your Baroness of Ceremonies can remind table hostesses to be asking the provided questions after women return from gathering decorating supplies. While the women are talking and decorating quietly play some background music.

Kitchen Couture Fashion Show

Once the decorating is done, it's time to show off those cool new aprons! Gather women together for a fashion show, where they'll get to wear their aprons for all to see.

Your fashion show should be high-energy fun. Don't just send the ladies to the front of the room, treat them like the Culinary Queens they are. Make it a fun fashion show they'll remember. Now's the time you need your royal court and drama team to rally women to participate. Your royal court, drama team, and greeters also can participate in the show. Once the ladies have seen

Helpful Hint

You may want a few extra tables or an area set aside where the ladies can set their aprons to dry while they work on their cookbook covers.

Another option with the cookbooks is to have your church name, women's ministry name, or event name printed on the cover.

Helpful Hint

For added fun, have each woman write a silly description of her apron on an index card. Have someone read these as if announcing the fashion show. Something like, "This apron, trimmed with pink feathers and sequins, won't last long in the kitchen. That's OK—because I'm only going to wear it while eating bonbons and watching movies!"

how well all of you do, they'll want to join in the fun. We've included several tracks on the CD-ROM to play while women strut their stuff.

Again, it's your job to set the tone in everything you do. So, when you have your royal court come out to show off their aprons, don't just walk across the stage. Think fashion show, think fun! You could even get the Countess of Tech to have lighting and a fog machine for the show.

Fashion Drama

Here's a drama to do before your fashion show that will really drive the message home about how unique and equally wonderful we all are.

Have 12 women come on stage, each one dressed differently. Include women of all ages, sizes, and ethnicities. Have them dressed in a variety of styles such as: a business woman, police officer, soccer player, a mom with a stroller, a trendy woman, a pregnant woman, a college student, and so on.

Each woman should carry a sign, with the writing side turned toward her so the audience can't see the message. After each woman is on stage, each woman will say one short sentence, such as: "I like ice cream," "I love to cook," "I don't like to cook at all," "I love to vacuum," "I hate to clean toilets," "My favorite color is pink," "I hate pink," "Sushi is my thing," "I am a vegetarian," and so on. Then after they have each said their one sentence, one at a time, they each turn over their signs in order to reveal Psalm 139:14: "Thank you for making me so wonderfully complex! Your workmanship is marvelous." This is a quick and easy skit to show that we are each unique—on the outside and on the inside, too, just the way God intended us to be.

Closing

Have the Baroness of Ceremonies close your event with a prayer and a reminder of what you've all learned together. She can encourage women by reminding them of how uniquely and marvelously made they are: "Thank you for making me so wonderfully complex! Your workmanship is marvelous" (Psalm 139:14). If God thinks we are marvelous, we need to think the same of ourselves. She should also remind women of the Proverbs 31 woman. The fun couture aprons and cookbooks can be a reminder to have a light-spirited attitude toward domestication. But, more importantly, remind women that the key to being a Proverbs 31 woman is the fear of the Lord. They don't need to be charming, beautiful, or Martha Stewart, they simply need to fear him and trust that he's made them marvelous.

*If you've enjoyed this out-of-the-box event, look for more innovative women's ministry resources at www.group .com/women. Still in the mood for food? Try **Girls' Night Out™ Party Kits: Dinner Around the World.** This party kit includes everything you need for a fun night with girlfriends—take a culinary journey around the world without leaving your home!*

Winter Wonderland

What could be more fun than hosting a women's Christmas event where the room is decorated as a winter wonderland with Christmas trees, snow, ice skates, and sleds? Add to that interactive activities in which women experience the wonder of Christmas. What is the wonder of Christmas? God sent his Son as *the* gift. It's the best gift we could ever receive or give. Help women to slow down from holiday bustle in order to unwrap the greatest present.

At your Winter Wonderland, women will participate in their own Christmas cooking show, they'll create Christmas topiaries, and they'll experience an interactive Christmas devotion that will help them appreciate God's incredible gift and bring the gift home to their friends and families.

Getting Started

∼ Recruiting for Winter Wonderland ∼

About 10 weeks before your Winter Wonderland event, you'll want to begin recruiting. This is a great event to invite others to join you. You can delegate all of these roles, or you can combine them depending on your team size. These are the different positions:

🎄 **The Director** of the event is the person who coordinates and directs the team. She'll make sure everyone is on the same page and moving in the same direction. She'll also be in charge of finances, making sure the budget is followed. This will probably be you!

🎄 **The Promotion Coordinator** will promote the event. She'll make announcements, distribute invitations, and hang posters. This person needs to be a positive, inviting person and comfortable speaking in front of a large group of people.

The Registration Coordinator will register each lady who signs up to come to the event and be in charge of the list of attendees and whether or not they've paid (if you decide to charge for the event). This team member needs to be organized, warm, and welcoming.

The Table Hostess Coordinator will direct the Table Hostesses. (More on these later!) She'll let them know what their role is and help them with any needs they may have. She needs to be diplomatic and able to direct a small group.

The Emcee will host the event. She'll welcome the women at the beginning, give directions to the women as the event unfolds, and lead the devotion. She should be upbeat, welcoming, be able to give instructions clearly, and be comfortable speaking in front of a large group.

The Decorator should be someone who has a creative flare. You know who this is, everyone wants her to come and help decorate her house! This person should not only be in charge of setting up the event but also cleaning up. She will need to recruit a team to help her on the day of the event.

The Craft Leader will lead women in making a holiday topiary. She should be skilled at and enthusiastic about crafts, able to give clear instructions, and comfortable speaking in front of a large group. She'll provide the supplies needed for the crafts.

The Christmas Cooking Show Leader will be in charge of the cooking activity women will participate in. She'll provide the supplies needed for each table and lead this activity. She should love cooking and be comfortable speaking in front of a group.

There are other roles that you may consider adding. For instance, if you would like to have a meal at the event, you'll need someone to coordinate this by either hiring a caterer or organizing a group of women to provide the food. You will at least want drinks for women. Choose a team member to be in charge of this. (Women will make desserts to eat during the Christmas Cooking Show.) To set the mood, you may want to have live music such as a worship team or carolers. Either way, you would need someone to coordinate this. If you have a large group, you'll need a Sound Coordinator to organize microphones or other sound equipment.

Depending on the size of your group, you may want to have your team take on more than one role. But remember, the idea for the Director is to delegate, delegate, delegate. Otherwise everyone's plate may become too full, and we all know what happens when we get to that point. Also it's great to have lots of women involved—it creates camaraderie and a sense of connectedness.

Timeline

 ### Eight weeks before your event

- Begin praying for your Winter Wonderland.

- Read through this chapter in its entirety.

- Recruit your event team.

- Estimate how many women will attend your event, using figures from previous retreats or women's events as a guide. This will help you finalize location details.

- Set a budget, determining how much your event team will have to work with.

Seven weeks before your event

- Meet with your event leaders. (You may want them to read this chapter before the meeting.) At this meeting:

  - Choose the event date.

  - Choose the location. (Read the Decorating and Setup section for what you'll need in a location.)

  - Go over role descriptions and this outline of your event.

  - Decide on publicity. (See the "Promoting Winter Wonderland" section and the CD-ROM.)

  - Decide whether you'll charge a participant's fee.

  - Decide whether you'll provide child care.

- Reserve the area where you've decided to host the event for the day of the event and the day before for setup.

Six weeks before your event

- Launch publicity.

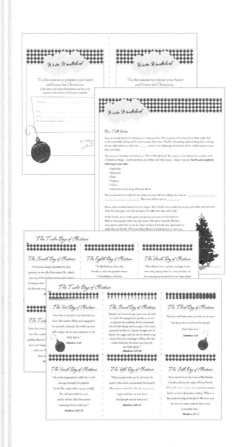

Four weeks before your event

- Continue publicity.

- Begin signing women up for your event.

- The Table Hostess Coordinator starts recruiting table hostesses.

- The Decorator recruits a team of helpers and begins planning decorations.

 Two weeks before your event

- Continue publicity and registration.

- The Craft Leader gathers supplies for the craft and prepares for demonstration.

- The Table Hostesses begin planning their tables.

- The Christmas Cooking Show Leader begins gathering supplies and planning her segment.

- Request any technical support you'll need for the event.

 The week of your event

- Don't forget to keep praying!

- Send an e-mail reminder to women.

- The Emcee reads through and prepares for the devotional.

The day of your event

- The Decorator and her team arrive early to decorate. (They may want to decorate the night before.)

- The event team arrives early to pray over the event, turn the music on, and troubleshoot any last-minute challenges.

- The Table Hostesses arrive early to decorate their tables.

(Adapt the following schedule to fit your plan. You may want to add a music program or a meal, or you may want to have a morning or evening event rather than an afternoon event.)

1:00 to 1:45 p.m.	Sound check, troubleshoot, and pray
1:45 to 2:00 p.m.	Registration and Welcome
2:00 to 2:30 p.m.	The Twelve Days of Christmas Devotion
2:30 to 3:00 p.m.	Making a Christmas Topiary

Helpful Hint

It's important to arrive early before an event begins. If you're still rushing around as guests arrive, it makes everyone feel uncomfortable and creates a sense of chaos. It's best if everyone is relaxed and ready when the guests arrive.

This is an important tip. It can set the tone of the event: Smiles, everyone, smiles!

3:00 to 3:45 p.m. . . . . Christmas Cooking Show

3:45 to 4:00 p.m. . . . . Closing prayer and farewell

The week after your event

- Send out thank you cards to your event team or have an appreciation party. Sincerely thank your event team. People want to be valued for their contributions!

Let's Get Planning!

Planning and Training for the Event

About seven weeks before your event, you'll want to plan a training meeting with your team. This allows everyone ample time to plan, especially since this event is during the holiday season which already in November gets to be very busy!

This training time should be fun and the idea is for everyone to catch the vision of the event and leave excited about the part they get to play. You'll want to give them an overview of what "Winter Wonderland" will look like. To get everyone in the mood, you could decorate the room with Christmas decorations, serve Christmas cookies, and have Christmas music playing in the background.

Here's a list of things you may want to hand out during your training session:

- lists of team members, their phone numbers, and their roles
- copies of the Table Hostess letter for all of the Table Hostesses (you'll find this on the CD-ROM)
- a proposed budget
- schedules of the event
- blank sheets of paper for taking notes
- pens

Don't forget to remind the ladies why they're doing what they are doing, which is not only to bring women together at a festive event to have some fun, but also to have an inspiring time, where they're challenged to grasp the wonder of Christmas. Go over event location, date, child care, decorating, and publicity.

Have fun casting the vision!

Promoting

Make sure the women of your church are as excited about your event as you are! Use these promoting tips to get you started.

- Make a verbal announcement during church services. When you do this, make sure you are upbeat, excited, and include all of the pertinent information. They'll need to know the when, where, and how of the event. Point out the cost and where to sign up. Don't forget to let the ladies know how much fun everyone is going to have. (Make those men jealous that this is only a women's event!)

- Use the clip art on the CD-ROM to create a PowerPoint announcement slide to show before services.

- Hand out or mail invitations. You can print invitations from the CD-ROM. It's always good to put something in their hands. Attach a small magnet to the back of the each invitation before you hand them out so the ladies can put them on their fridge as a reminder to sign up and attend.

- Use the clip art from the CD-ROM to create a bulletin insert or use the invitation as a bulletin insert.

- Posters are a great way to create excitement about this event. Create posters using the clip art on the CD-ROM. Hang them in the ladies' restrooms and around the church in authorized areas. You could even attach them to a wooden stake and put them in the landscape where people are most likely to see them.

Registration

About six weeks before Winter Wonderland, begin registration. The ladies will already be excited about signing up, thanks to your Promotion Coordinator.

If you are charging for this event, decide if you'll sell tickets that they present at the door or if you'll have a master list with names. (A list with names is a sure bet, as sometimes in our busy schedules tickets can be misplaced.)

Helpful Hint

To catch the ladies' attention for the announcement, a skit is always a fun idea. You can do this yourself or invite those drama queens to help you!

It's best if you have the ladies pay as they sign up so you have an exact count and they have a vested interest and are more likely to show up the day of the event.

The registration table needs to be in a visible area and it would add excitement about the event if decorated. You could have a small, lit Christmas tree, Christmas candy, or Christmas cookies. And Christmas background music would add merriment as the women register.

Registration can get a little hectic as the women sign up, but remember to always greet the ladies with a smile and show them God's love. You'll be the first person they interact with for this event. You are the first face of Winter Wonderland, so—make it a smiling one!

The Table Hostesses

Your Table Hostesses will add a fun, creative element to your event and also help add a lot of the decorations. Your Table Hostess Coordinator will recruit a Table Hostess for each table. These women will decorate their tables as they like, according to the Winter Wonderland theme. They play an important role at the table, too. Each one will host the ladies at her table during the event, making sure each guest feels welcome and involved.

Every table will be different and will represent the Table Hostess's idea of a Winter Wonderland. Hostesses could go for a Christmas village theme, an all blue and white theme, a snowman theme, a sledding theme, a nativity theme, a stocking theme—the sky is the limit. Encourage women to be creative!

When the guests arrive, they'll all walk around and tour the tables. It'll bring another layer of wonder to the room. You can even award prizes to the Table Hostesses for the best of theme, the most elegant, and the most original. The Table Hostess Coordinator will direct the Table Hostesses. She'll help them with any needs that come up and will want to make sure everyone has read their Table Hostess letter and fully understands her role. (You'll find a sample Table Hostess letter on the CD-ROM.) It will be the Table Hostess Coordinator's responsibility to recruit judges for the table awards and to award the prizes if you choose to do this. (Coordinate this with the Director and the Emcee. Typically during the end of the program or a meal is a good time for the winners to be announced.)

Decorating and Setup

Any time you have an event, you want ambience. So therefore you've gotta decorate! And at Winter Wonderland, just the title alone takes you to

Helpful Hint
If decorating isn't your flare, ask the Decorating Coordinator for help. She's probably itching to get started decorating already!

Helpful Hint
When Winter Wonderland was done at a church in California, the women loved this part of Winter Wonderland. And women really went all out. There were even ice sculptures! And everyone was so excited to see who would win. At the end of the event, women already wanted to sign up to be Table Hostesses for the next year and were already planning their creations!

another place. You want to create an experience for the ladies as they walk in, so they see, smell, hear, and touch your Winter Wonderland.

You can choose to set up your location several ways. There are three elements to your event: the Twelve Days of Christmas devotion, the Christmas Topiary craft, and the Christmas Cooking Show.

The devotion can be led from the front of the room or stage. The Emcee will need a table set up for her to set the gifts she'll create on.

For the Christmas Topiary craft, one woman will lead the craft from the front while the women follow along making the craft at tables. It's a good idea to have a separate room or area set up for this, if possible. Depending on how extravagantly the Table Hostesses festoon the tables, there may not be room on the tables for craft supplies. (If you choose to simply have a woman demonstrate the craft and not have the ladies make it alongside her, set up a table at the front for this.)

For the Christmas Cooking Show, you'll want another area or room of tables for the women to cook at. Have a table at the front of the cooking area for the Christmas Cooking Show Leader. (Again, if you decide to simply have a woman demonstrate a dessert for the ladies to eat and not have the ladies cook with her, set up a table for the Christmas Cooking Show Leader at the front.)

If you have a stage, start your decorating here. If you don't, create a space at the front of the room where everyone can see. If space allows on the stage, begin creating a winter wonderland scene. You can use one or several Christmas trees lit up with white lights. Lots of imitation snow on the trees and all around the bottom of the trees brings winter right into the room. You can then begin filling in with sleds, ice skates, snowshoes, a snowman (not real of course!) and anything else that reminds you of a winter wonderland.

A great way to create a festive atmosphere is to have things hanging from the ceiling. For your Winter Wonderland, snowflakes would be perfect. You could either make these yourself or purchase them at any store that has Christmas decorations. White Christmas lights would add another layer of ornamentation. Draping these across the room would add a fun element.

After you've decorated the stage and have things hanging from the ceiling, it's now time to look at the entry. You should stage a scene near the registration table where the women first come in. First impressions are everything! This could be very elaborate or as simple as one snow dusted Christmas tree.

Helpful Hint

If you are planning on using white Christmas lights as your primary source of lighting, make sure you have spotlights or some other lighting for the stage so that it can be clearly seen.

Tuck Christmas trees here and there around the room, so as to create the right atmosphere. This doesn't have to cost you anything. You can ask to borrow Christmas trees from all of the ladies on the team. (You could even borrow trees from a nursery.) And don't worry about the trees matching. Different shapes, sizes and styles will add interest to the room. Don't forget to dust imitation snow all around. Snow, snow and more snow, is the moral to this story!

The ladies will be sitting at tables for this event. The Table Hostesses will be decorating these.

If you are having food, coordinate with the person who is in charge of this as you decorate. If there is a buffet table, you may want to provide table-cloths, a Christmas tree centerpiece and add a garland.

It's important that you bring in the right smells for this event. Of course, it needs to smell like a winter wonderland! Try bringing in some real ever-greens, even if it's just some branches that you gather from the ground off of a Christmas tree lot. The other thing you can do is to have candles, pot-pourri, or use an air spray to bring in a Christmas scent.

Walking Through Your Winter Wonderland

When women arrive, make sure they're warmly welcomed, and then let them know they can wander around your Winter Wonderland, appreciating all the Table Hostesses hard work! If you're serving a meal or hosting a music program, this would be a good time to do it. Once ladies have settled in, begin with the Twelve Days of Christmas Devotion.

The Twelve Days of Christmas Devotion

The Emcee will prepare this devotion for women to experience together at your event, and they'll be able to take the devotion home for friends or family. For each of the twelve days of Christmas, there are verses from the Christmas story, which will be wrapped in gifts. These verses are on the CD-ROM for you to print out and give to each woman. Each woman will

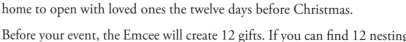

take home a handout so she can create Twelve Days of Christmas gifts at home to open with loved ones the twelve days before Christmas.

Before your event, the Emcee will create 12 gifts. If you can find 12 nesting boxes that fit into one another, it would be a great touch. The Emcee will cut out each Scripture reference and place it in a small box and then wrap it. Make the gifts beautiful—women will be unwrapping the most beautiful gift ever given! Make sure to label each gift 1 through 12.

Open your event and enthusiastically welcome all of the ladies. Let everyone know the agenda for the day; then pray and welcome the Lord to join you and ask him to bless your time together. Then begin:

I love Christmas; it's my favorite time of the year. It's the time we celebrate the birth of our Savior. Our theme for today is "Winter Wonderland." We want to share with you the wonder of Christmas.

At your tables, share with one another or with a partner your favorite gift you ever received and why it was so special to you. Pause several minutes for women to discuss. Then say:

Sometimes it seems like Christmas becomes all about the gifts. But that makes sense because the Christmas story is all about the greatest gift that's ever been given.

Today, we're going to experience unwrapping God's gift together.

Ask for three volunteers to come to the front and unwrap the first, second, and third gifts and read the verses inside to the group:

> *Now this is how Jesus the Messiah was born. His mother, Mary, was engaged to be married to Joseph. But while she was still a virgin, she became pregnant by the Holy Spirit. Joseph, her fiancé, being a just man, decided to break the engagement quietly, so as not to disgrace her publicly. As he considered this, he fell asleep, and an angel of the Lord appeared to him in a dream. "Joseph, son of David," the angel said, "do not be afraid to go ahead with your marriage to Mary. For the child within her has been conceived by the Holy Spirit" (Matthew 1:18-20).*

Then say: **If I were Mary, that would have been about the last gift I would have expected from God. It would have been quite an unbelievable surprise! Turn to a partner at your table, and talk about these questions:**

- **What's the most unbelievable gift God (or someone else) has ever given you?**

- **Has God or someone else ever surprised you with a gift—maybe even one that didn't seem like a "gift" at the time?**

Then ask for three more volunteers to open the third, fourth, and fifth gifts and read the Scriptures:

> *"And she will have a son, and you are to name him Jesus, for he will save his people from their sins. All of this happened to fulfill the Lord's message through his prophet:*
>
> *'Look! The virgin will conceive a child!*
> *She will give birth to a son,*
> *and he will be called Immanuel*
> *(meaning, God is with us).'*
> *When Joseph woke up, he did what the angel of the Lord commanded. He brought Mary home to be his wife, she remained a virgin until her son was born. And Joseph named him Jesus"* (Matthew 1:21-25).

SAY: **This message is the promise of the greatest gift, which God has been planning for centuries. The promise is that Jesus will save us from our sins. God saw our need for a Savior, that we had sinned and separated ourselves from him. There was nothing we could do—no amount of good works—that could reunite us with him. So he sent the ultimate gift, his very Son, to save us from our sins through his sacrifice.**

Close your eyes, and think about God planning out this gift for you. Contemplate the great love for you he must have in preparing such a gift. Think of a parent and the great care they take in wrapping a present for their child before Christmas, and the excitement and joy they have in giving it. Now picture God as the parent, delighted for the gift he's giving you. Pause.

With a partner, discuss how you feel to think that the God of the Universe planned and delivered such an incredible gift for you, out of his love for you. Pause.

Ask for three volunteers to come and open the sixth, seventh, and eighth gifts and read the Scriptures:

> *Jesus was born in the town of Bethlehem in Judea, during the reign of King Herod. About that time some wise men from eastern lands arrived in Jerusalem, asking, "Where is the newborn king of the Jews? We have seen his star as it arose, and we have come to worship him." Herod was deeply disturbed by their question, as was all of Jerusalem. He called a meeting of the leading priests and teachers of religious law. "Where did the prophets say the Messiah would be born?" he asked them.*
>
> *"In Bethlehem," they said, "for this is what the prophet wrote:*
> *'O Bethlehem of Judah,*

Helpful Hint

If you have around 12 tables, you could hand out one gift to each table to unwrap together and read the Scriptures to the group.

you are not just a lowly village in Judah,
for a ruler will come from you
who will be the shepherd for my people Israel' " (Matthew 2:1-6).

After the volunteers have finished reading, say: **The second part of God's gift in Jesus is, not only that he would be our Savior, but that he would also be our Shepherd. A shepherd is there each day, lovingly guiding his charges and keeping them safe. Turn to a partner and discuss what it means to you that not only is Jesus your Savior but also your daily shepherd.** Pause.

Ask for volunteers to come and open the remaining four presents and have them read the Scriptures:

> *"Then Herod sent a private message to the wise men, asking them to come see him. At this meeting he learned the exact time when they first saw the star. Then he told them, "Go to Bethlehem and search carefully for the child. And when you find him, come back and tell me so that I can go and worship him, too!" After this interview the wise men went their way. Once again the star appeared to them, guiding them to Bethlehem. It went ahead of them and stopped over the place where the child was. When they saw the star, they were filled with joy! They entered the house where the child and his mother, Mary, were, and they fell down before him and worshiped him. Then they opened their treasure chests and gave him gifts of gold, frankincense, and myrrh. But when it was time to leave, they went home another way, because God had warned them in a dream not to return to Herod"* (Matthew 2:7-12).

After the volunteers have read, say: **Imagine being those wise men. When they experienced the wonder of what God had done, they were filled with joy, and they worshipped God. That's why we're here today and that's why we're so jubilant at this time of year—to worship God for the wonder of his gift and the joy he's given us!**

Turn to a partner and tell them about the time you were most filled with joy. It may have been when your kids were born, a favorite vacation, or a time with God. Pause.

Close your eyes again, and contemplate the gift that God has given you. He loves you, he saved you, and he wants to be your shepherd. Pause.

Ask God to fill you with new joy this season as you celebrate his gift. Take a few moments to pray silently to God, worshipping him and thanking him for his gift.

Close in prayer: **God, your gift to us in Jesus is more than we could ever**

have asked for or imagined. Thank you for the love you have for us and that you've been wrapping this present for us, planning to give it to us, and hoping we'll open it. We worship you for your love and your sacrifice. Help us to be filled with your joy this holiday season so that we can share your gift with those around us. In Jesus' name, amen.

After the devotional, tell women how to experience this gift at home. Tell them that there are handouts for each of them to take home. They can create gifts to unwrap together with friends, family, or their children. They'll open one gift a day, beginning on the 14th of December.

Depending on whom they intend to give the gifts to, they can include small gifts in each present. Christmas cookies or fudge could be placed in each gift. If the gifts are for children, small toys or pieces of candy could be included in each gift. If the gifts are for a husband, women could include love notes in the boxes. If it's for friends, it could be chocolates or pictures. Each day, women can open the box with family or friends and discuss the story of the Christmas gift. For each day, she should discuss with them what that verse means to them or reminds them of. Reading the Christmas story may even become a holiday tradition!

The Emcee should now dismiss women to the craft-making area to make the Christmas Topiaries.

Christmas Topiary Craft

This is a fun, easy craft that women can make together to decorate their homes with or give as gifts. Provide supplies at each table for each woman to make one.

Supplies

Here's what you'll need for each woman:

Red and white mints, gumdrops, or hard candies

Glue gun and glue sticks

Terra-cotta pot

Styrofoam ball (not to exceed the diameter of your pot)

Sturdy candy stick, such as a thick red and white candy cane or dowel

Sugar or sand

Ribbon

Making the Topiary

- Glue the candy stick into the bottom of your pot.

- Fill the pot with sand or sugar, up to about 1 inch from the top. Cover this with red and white mints or gumdrops.

- Place the Styrofoam ball on the candy stick pushing it on to the stick about 1 inch deep.

- Starting at the top of the ball, glue your candy on. Cover the entire ball, alternating colors to create a pattern or design as desired.

- When the Styrofoam ball is completely covered, add the final addition of a decorative bow on the topiary.

You can choose several color schemes for your topiary: All red and white mints with a red ribbon. Bright, multicolored gumdrops with a green ribbon. All blue and white mints with a white or blue ribbon. While women work to glue their candies on, the Craft Leader should encourage the women to discuss fun topics, such as favorite Christmas memories or what their favorite family tradition is.

Christmas Cooking Show

Have you stood in your kitchen many a day, spatula in hand, pretending to be Julia Child? Well, get ready to have some fun! In your lively Christmas Cooking Show, women will make desserts to share with one another. Each table will have different dessert ingredients, and it will be up to each table to come up with a Christmas dessert together. They'll name their recipe, and write the instructions down on recipe cards you, the Cooking Show Leader, provide. This is a great way to get easy holiday cooking ideas, have fun with each other, and eat a tasty dessert. But first, you'll start the Christmas Cooking Show with a demonstration of you own.

At your front table, you'll demonstrate a simple, layered Christmas dessert. For this recipe, you'll need a large bowl, a mixing spoon, and a serving spoon. Tell women that this is an easy dessert to make together with the family, and a holiday treat that kids will look forward to making together each year. Demonstrate making the dessert as women watch. Here's the recipe:

Strawberry Dream

32 ounces unsweetened frozen strawberries, thawed

8 ounces whipped topping, thawed

1 cup chopped walnuts

1 cup semi-sweet chocolate chips

Gently mix ingredients together in a large bowl. Serve immediately or refrigerate until ready to serve. Enjoy!

After your demonstration, tell women that it's their turn to put on their chef's hats. Tell women that they'll have 15 to 20 minutes to create their own holiday dessert masterpiece. Tell them to name them and write the recipes down.

At each table, have different ingredients that can be put together to create a simple dessert. Have the tools necessary, such as a pie plate, a mixing bowl, a whisk, and a spoon. Here are some ideas:

For a Tiramisu-like creation:

1 cup espresso (labeled so they know what it is)

1 package ladyfingers

1 package marscapone cream

½ cup powdered sugar

chocolate shavings

cocoa powder

For a layered pie dessert:

1 prepared graham cracker crust

1 container whipped topping

one 14-ounce container chocolate pudding/pie filling

2 bananas

candy bar crumbles

For a fruit pie dessert:

1 large pre-made sugar cookie crust

1 8-ounce package cream cheese

½ cup sugar

kiwis, strawberries, and other fruits

Helpful Hint

Feel free to substitute your own easy recipe here. Make sure it's one that you can make and serve immediately, such as Tiramisu (no baking).

Make sure to have plates, spoons, and napkins at each table for taste testing!

If time and budget don't allow for an all-out Cooking Show, simply have the Christmas Cooking Show Leader demonstrate one dessert that the women will then share together.

Have fun creating various groups of ingredients to set at each table. Here's a general list of ingredients that you could set out at tables, and let the ladies' creativity be their guide:

fruit preserves	whipping cream
flaked coconut	bananas, or other fresh fruits
chocolate chips	cookie crusts
butterscotch chips	pre-made graham cracker crusts
peanut butter	ladyfingers
chocolate pudding/pie filling	crumbled candy bars
cherry pie filling	cookies, whole or crumbled

While women are cooking together, have them discuss what their favorite Christmas dessert or cookie is. Encourage them to make sure each lady is involved. After the time is up, get women's attention. Let them know that they can now tour the other tables to see what everyone came up with. Encourage them to serve themselves from whichever desserts are their favorites. If you want to add another layer of fun to your Christmas Cooking Show, ask tables to each present their desserts to the other ladies.

After women are done nibbling on their desserts, the Emcee will close your time together.

Closing and Farewell

Thank women for coming to your Winter Wonderland. Say: **Wasn't that fun? You all are some excellent cooks! That was a rich treat! In Psalm 63:5 the Psalmist says of God, "You satisfy me more than the richest feast. I will praise you with songs of joy." God is more rich and satisfying than the best of Christmas feasts—they're just a hint of how wondrous he is. He's offered us a gift in his Son, forgiveness from our sins. Let's take a moment to praise him for that.**

Dear God, thank you so much for this season when we remember the gift you've given us. We praise you for your Son and we want to open your gift. Your gift satisfies us more than the richest of foods. We want to praise you for all the joy you've brought to us. Help us this season, when surrounded by the gifts and feasts, to be reminded of your wonder and your great gift. In Jesus' name, amen.

If there are women who've never heard of the gift of Jesus, offer to stick around to tell them more about it. This is a perfect opportunity to lead women into a relationship with the Lord. It would be a good idea to have an unthreatening place for these ladies to go after you dismiss.

Helpful Hint
As soon as the Emcee leaves the stage, begin playing background Christmas music. It just continues the festive atmosphere.